READING THE
Bible
COVER TO COVER
in 365 Days

DISCOVERING GOD'S HEART THROUGH HIS WORD

ANDREA LENDE

Copyright

ALSO BY ANDREA LENDE:

90 Day Prayer Journal: Drawing Closer to God Through Prayer

Life After Lupus: What's Your Autoimmune Name?

God is Still Almighty: 90 Daily Devotions

Coffee and a Prayer: 90 Peaceful Prayers

God's Whispers and Melodies: A Heart Transformed through Music and Lyrics

A Mother's Love: Leaving a Legacy through Poetry and Prayer

ACKNOWLEDGMENTS

Thank you, Robin Elliott and Becky Connell, for spending the year reading the Bible with me. Sometimes we stumbled along, but we made great strides, and encouraged one another through its entirety. You have both been such an inspiration in making this project come to life.

Thank you, Becky Connell, for working so diligently on the reading schedule, correcting my mistakes, and creating multiple mathematical systems for reading the Bible in 365 days.

Thank you, Aprille Vasu, for being so enthusiastic about reading the Bible that it pushed this project along at lightning speed! Thank you for your lovely endorsement!

Thank you, Emily Moore, for your encouragement, counsel, and for your inspiring endorsement!

Thank you, John Andrew Lende, for working with me on this project and encouraging me through its completion.

DEDICATION

To, Aprille Vasu, who inspired me to organize over ten years of reading the Bible into a system that can be used to bless many as they embark on their own journey to discover the heart of God through His Word. May God continue to bless you, Aprille, as you seek Him.

INTRODUCTION

Welcome to this journey! A journey into God's Word that has transformed my life and will likely transform yours as well.

Most of us have participated in Bible studies where we study one book of the Bible at a time. We don't often consider reading the Bible from cover to cover because it seems like a daunting task. We wonder where to start; we question whether we are doing it "correctly;" and if we are honest with ourselves, we have doubts about whether we will be able to fully commit and complete such a massive endeavor.

If we do start, most of us begin reading in Genesis which is a reasonable place to begin. We give up reading somewhere in Numbers or Deuteronomy because we become lost in all the numbers or disillusioned with the struggle of the Israelites. However, there is a balanced way to read the Bible cover to cover that I've found which has kept me and others engaged and inspired to continue reading until the end. First, I'd like to share the reason I started reading the Bible this way many years ago and still do today.

Some years back, my finances didn't allow me to purchase Bible study materials. God called me to simply sit with Him and the Bible and seek Him in His Word. It was a year or two of discovery: discovering God's heart as I read about Him. Before I began, He showed me the way to read the Bible cover to cover in a way that helped me stay engaged with Him throughout the whole Book with the desire to come back and read it over and over again. I'm so excited to share the process with you!

This program encompasses reading books in both the Old Testament and New Testament every day. Please know that whatever timeline you design for yourself is perfect for you. God meets you exactly where you are. There is no requirement to read the Bible in a year, however, the schedule to do so is provided for you if that is your desire.

WHAT YOU WILL ACCOMPLISH ACCORDING TO THE READING SCHEDULE

First four Gospels: 4 times

Acts – Revelation: 2 times

Psalms and Proverbs: 2 times

Genesis – Malachi: 1 time

If rereading these books ever stops making sense to you, you most assuredly can decide to stop. If at any time you want to simply read the chapters you haven't read, you can choose to read only the new chapters. I have found reading according to the schedule in this book provides relevancy and insights that I could not have predicted had I not read the Old and New Testament chapters simultaneously. I have also found it provides a much deeper dimension to reading the Word which has been pivotal for me on my journey to discovering God's heart.

HOW TO RECEIVE THE MOST OUT OF READING THE BIBLE COVER TO COVER:

- Read the introduction to each new book to learn about the author and gain context of the time period. I read out of the Amplified Bible for better understanding and meaning. Whatever Bible you choose to read is the perfect version for you.

- Pray for God's gentle whispers to speak to your heart as you read.

- Keep your heart open for encouragement as you read God's Word.

- Consider how to apply the lesson you read to your daily life.

- Ask God to help you receive all He has for you to receive. We don't often allow ourselves to receive all the promises we read about. The promises in God's Word are meant for us today just as they were meant for God's people thousands of years ago.

- Highlight meaningful verses and stories as you read them. The desire to highlight the verses and stories that stir your heart is one way you hear God's gentle whispers.

- Write down your favorite verses. Again, the verses that speak to you is one way you hear God's voice. It's a gentle whisper from Him for you to treasure. There is a place for you to write your favorite verse in this book. You can also write verses on notecards. I suggest keeping the notecards with you throughout the day and referring to them often. Allow the Word of God to continue to speak to your heart as you move through your day. At the end of the year, you will have at least 365 notecards of verses that

God has whispered to you. You may have even memorized many of those verses! Learning Scripture reaps tremendous fruit in God's kingdom.

- You may want to consider having a separate composition book or notebook to take notes in as you read. As I read Scripture, God nudges me to write down verses, thoughts, ideas He gives me while reading (inspiration), and other such things that are noteworthy. If I don't take time to write them down as I read, they are quickly forgotten.

There is an acrostic provided to help you reflect on the daily reading passages. It is formed from the word HEAR. Below is an example of what you'll find in this book.

H: _____
What gentle whisper did you hear as you read today?

E: _____
How did the passages encourage you?

A: _____
How can you apply what you learned in your day today?

R: _____
What do you need to receive from God? His love, mercy, grace, comfort, or something else?

A daily prayer is also provided which coincides with the acrostic above. Feel free to say your own prayer if you prefer. The daily prayer in this book is:

Lord, help me hear Your gentle whispers as I read Your Word. Encourage me as I learn more about Your heart. Help me apply what I learn and act according to Your will. And help me receive all You have for me to receive from You today. In Jesus' name, Amen.

HOW TO UTILIZE THIS STUDY INDEPENDENTLY OR IN A GROUP

This study is perfect to engage in independently or with a group. I have done both and found both to be rewarding in different ways. If you love to work independently, this reading schedule is designed for you to work alone and glean magnificent Truths in God's Word. If you want to embark on this journey with others, you will also be wonderfully blessed. When working in a group, I suggest meeting weekly to discuss the reading for the week, share your favorite Bible verses with each other and talk about how you've applied what you've learned throughout the week. Lastly, no study would be complete without talking about how God met you in the Scriptures and taught you a new Truth. Both independent and group studies are fruitful and lovely ways to enjoy this journey.

You may be a seasoned Bible reader, Bible teacher, or a beginning Bible reader. Wherever you are, reading God's Word consistently draws us closer to Him. There are always new things to learn and new ways to experience God through His Word. There are also new perspectives to glean depending on the season of your life. As soon as I finish reading the Bible cover to cover, I begin again. I hope you will consider reading the Word an activity you engage in regularly throughout your life.

May God bless you as you embark on this journey and discover more of Who God is as you seek to know His heart through reading His Word cover to cover.

DAILY PRAYER

Lord, help me hear Your gentle whispers as I read Your Word. Encourage me as I learn more about Your heart. Help me apply what I learn and act according to Your will. And help me receive all You have for me to receive from You today. In Jesus' name, Amen.

DAY 1:

Matthew: Chapter 1
Acts: Chapter 1
Genesis: Chapters 1-2
Psalm 1

H: _____
What gentle whisper did you hear as you read today?

E: _____
How did the passages encourage you?

A: _____
How can you apply what you learned in your day today?

R: _____
What do you need to receive from God? His love, mercy, grace, comfort, or something else?

Write your favorite verse from today's reading here:

_____

_____

DAY 2:

Matthew: Chapter 2
Acts: Chapter 2
Genesis: Chapters 3-4
Psalm 2

H: _____
What gentle whisper did you hear as you read today?

E: _____
How did the passages encourage you?

A: _____
How can you apply what you learned in your day today?

R: _____
What do you need to receive from God? His love, mercy, grace, comfort, or something else?

Write your favorite verse from today's reading here:

_____

_____

DAILY PRAYER

Lord, help me hear Your gentle whispers as I read Your Word. Encourage me as I learn more about Your heart. Help me apply what I learn and act according to Your will. And help me receive all You have for me to receive from You today. In Jesus' name, Amen.

DAY 3:

Matthew: Chapter 3
Acts: Chapter 3
Genesis: Chapters 5-6
Psalm 3

H: _____
What gentle whisper did you hear as you read today?

E: _____
How did the passages encourage you?

A: _____
How can you apply what you learned in your day today?

R: _____
What do you need to receive from God? His love, mercy, grace, comfort, or something else?

Write your favorite verse from today's reading here:

_____
_____

DAY 4:

Matthew: Chapter 4
Acts: Chapter 4
Genesis: Chapters 7-8
Psalm 4

H: _____
What gentle whisper did you hear as you read today?

E: _____
How did the passages encourage you?

A: _____
How can you apply what you learned in your day today?

R: _____
What do you need to receive from God? His love, mercy, grace, comfort, or something else?

Write your favorite verse from today's reading here:

_____
_____

DAILY PRAYER

Lord, help me hear Your gentle whispers as I read Your Word. Encourage me as I learn more about Your heart. Help me apply what I learn and act according to Your will. And help me receive all You have for me to receive from You today. In Jesus' name, Amen.

DAY 5:

Matthew: Chapter 5
Acts: Chapter 5
Genesis: Chapters 9-10
Psalm 5

H: _____
What gentle whisper did you hear as you read today?

E: _____
How did the passages encourage you?

A: _____
How can you apply what you learned in your day today?

R: _____
What do you need to receive from God? His love, mercy, grace, comfort, or something else?

Write your favorite verse from today's reading here:

_____

_____

DAY 6:

Matthew: Chapter 6
Acts: Chapter 6
Genesis: Chapters 11-12
Psalm 6

H: _____
What gentle whisper did you hear as you read today?

E: _____
How did the passages encourage you?

A: _____
How can you apply what you learned in your day today?

R: _____
What do you need to receive from God? His love, mercy, grace, comfort, or something else?

Write your favorite verse from today's reading here:

_____

_____

DAILY PRAYER

Lord, help me hear Your gentle whispers as I read Your Word. Encourage me as I learn more about Your heart. Help me apply what I learn and act according to Your will. And help me receive all You have for me to receive from You today. In Jesus' name, Amen.

DAY 7:

Matthew: Chapter 7
Acts: Chapter 7
Genesis: Chapters 13-14
Psalm 7

H: _____
What gentle whisper did you hear as you read today?

E: _____
How did the passages encourage you?

A: _____
How can you apply what you learned in your day today?

R: _____
What do you need to receive from God? His love, mercy, grace, comfort, or something else?

Write your favorite verse from today's reading here:

_____
_____

DAY 8:

Matthew: Chapter 8
Acts: Chapter 8
Genesis: Chapters 15-16
Psalm 8

H: _____
What gentle whisper did you hear as you read today?

E: _____
How did the passages encourage you?

A: _____
How can you apply what you learned in your day today?

R: _____
What do you need to receive from God? His love, mercy, grace, comfort, or something else?

Write your favorite verse from today's reading here:

_____
_____

DAILY PRAYER

Lord, help me hear Your gentle whispers as I read Your Word. Encourage me as I learn more about Your heart. Help me apply what I learn and act according to Your will. And help me receive all You have for me to receive from You today. In Jesus' name, Amen.

DAY 9:

Matthew: Chapter 9
Acts: Chapter 9
Genesis: Chapters 17-18
Psalm 9

H: _____
What gentle whisper did you hear as you read today?

E: _____
How did the passages encourage you?

A: _____
How can you apply what you learned in your day today?

R: _____
What do you need to receive from God? His love, mercy, grace, comfort, or something else?

Write your favorite verse from today's reading here:

_____

_____

DAY 10:

Matthew: Chapter 10
Acts: Chapter 10
Genesis: Chapters 19-20
Psalm 10

H: _____
What gentle whisper did you hear as you read today?

E: _____
How did the passages encourage you?

A: _____
How can you apply what you learned in your day today?

R: _____
What do you need to receive from God? His love, mercy, grace, comfort, or something else?

Write your favorite verse from today's reading here:

_____

_____

DAILY PRAYER

Lord, help me hear Your gentle whispers as I read Your Word. Encourage me as I learn more about Your heart. Help me apply what I learn and act according to Your will. And help me receive all You have for me to receive from You today. In Jesus' name, Amen.

DAY 11:

Matthew: Chapter 11
Acts: Chapter 11
Genesis: Chapters 21-22
Psalm 11

H: _____
What gentle whisper did you hear as you read today?

E: _____
How did the passages encourage you?

A: _____
How can you apply what you learned in your day today?

R: _____
What do you need to receive from God? His love, mercy, grace, comfort, or something else?

Write your favorite verse from today's reading here:

_____
_____

DAY 12:

Matthew: Chapter 12
Acts: Chapter 12
Genesis: Chapters 23-24
Psalm 12

H: _____
What gentle whisper did you hear as you read today?

E: _____
How did the passages encourage you?

A: _____
How can you apply what you learned in your day today?

R: _____
What do you need to receive from God? His love, mercy, grace, comfort, or something else?

Write your favorite verse from today's reading here:

_____
_____

DAILY PRAYER

Lord, help me hear Your gentle whispers as I read Your Word. Encourage me as I learn more about Your heart. Help me apply what I learn and act according to Your will. And help me receive all You have for me to receive from You today. In Jesus' name, Amen.

DAY 13:

Matthew: Chapter 13
Acts: Chapter 13
Genesis: Chapters 25-26
Psalm 13

H: _____
What gentle whisper did you hear as you read today?

E: _____
How did the passages encourage you?

A: _____
How can you apply what you learned in your day today?

R: _____
What do you need to receive from God? His love, mercy, grace, comfort, or something else?

Write your favorite verse from today's reading here:

_____

_____

DAY 14:

Matthew: Chapter 14
Acts: Chapter 14
Genesis: Chapters 27-28
Psalm 14

H: _____
What gentle whisper did you hear as you read today?

E: _____
How did the passages encourage you?

A: _____
How can you apply what you learned in your day today?

R: _____
What do you need to receive from God? His love, mercy, grace, comfort, or something else?

Write your favorite verse from today's reading here:

_____

_____

DAILY PRAYER

Lord, help me hear Your gentle whispers as I read Your Word. Encourage me as I learn more about Your heart. Help me apply what I learn and act according to Your will. And help me receive all You have for me to receive from You today. In Jesus' name, Amen.

DAY 15:

Matthew: Chapter 15
Acts: Chapter 15
Genesis: Chapters 29-30
Psalm 15

H: _____
What gentle whisper did you hear as you read today?

E: _____
How did the passages encourage you?

A: _____
How can you apply what you learned in your day today?

R: _____
What do you need to receive from God? His love, mercy, grace, comfort, or something else?

Write your favorite verse from today's reading here:

_____

_____

DAY 16:

Matthew: Chapter 16
Acts: Chapter 16
Genesis: Chapters 31-32
Psalm 16

H: _____
What gentle whisper did you hear as you read today?

E: _____
How did the passages encourage you?

A: _____
How can you apply what you learned in your day today?

R: _____
What do you need to receive from God? His love, mercy, grace, comfort, or something else?

Write your favorite verse from today's reading here:

_____

_____

DAILY PRAYER

Lord, help me hear Your gentle whispers as I read Your Word. Encourage me as I learn more about Your heart. Help me apply what I learn and act according to Your will. And help me receive all You have for me to receive from You today. In Jesus' name, Amen.

DAY 17:

Matthew: Chapter 17
Acts: Chapter 17
Genesis: Chapters 33-34
Psalm 17

H: _____
What gentle whisper did you hear as you read today?

E: _____
How did the passages encourage you?

A: _____
How can you apply what you learned in your day today?

R: _____
What do you need to receive from God? His love, mercy, grace, comfort, or something else?

Write your favorite verse from today's reading here:

_____

_____

DAY 18:

Matthew: Chapter 18
Acts: Chapter 18
Genesis: Chapters 35-36
Psalm 18

H: _____
What gentle whisper did you hear as you read today?

E: _____
How did the passages encourage you?

A: _____
How can you apply what you learned in your day today?

R: _____
What do you need to receive from God? His love, mercy, grace, comfort, or something else?

Write your favorite verse from today's reading here:

_____

_____

DAILY PRAYER

Lord, help me hear Your gentle whispers as I read Your Word. Encourage me as I learn more about Your heart. Help me apply what I learn and act according to Your will. And help me receive all You have for me to receive from You today. In Jesus' name, Amen.

DAY 19:

Matthew: Chapter 19
Acts: Chapter 19
Genesis: Chapters 37-38
Psalm 19

H: _____
What gentle whisper did you hear as you read today?

E: _____
How did the passages encourage you?

A: _____
How can you apply what you learned in your day today?

R: _____
What do you need to receive from God? His love, mercy, grace, comfort, or something else?

Write your favorite verse from today's reading here:

_____

_____

DAY 20:

Matthew: Chapter 20
Acts: Chapter 20
Genesis: Chapters 39-40
Psalm 20

H: _____
What gentle whisper did you hear as you read today?

E: _____
How did the passages encourage you?

A: _____
How can you apply what you learned in your day today?

R: _____
What do you need to receive from God? His love, mercy, grace, comfort, or something else?

Write your favorite verse from today's reading here:

_____

_____

DAILY PRAYER

Lord, help me hear Your gentle whispers as I read Your Word. Encourage me as I learn more about Your heart. Help me apply what I learn and act according to Your will. And help me receive all You have for me to receive from You today. In Jesus' name, Amen.

DAY 21:

Matthew: Chapter 21
Acts: Chapter 21
Genesis: Chapters 41-42
Psalm 21

H: _____
What gentle whisper did you hear as you read today?

E: _____
How did the passages encourage you?

A: _____
How can you apply what you learned in your day today?

R: _____
What do you need to receive from God? His love, mercy, grace, comfort, or something else?

Write your favorite verse from today's reading here:

_____

_____

DAY 22:

Matthew: Chapter 22
Acts: Chapter 22
Genesis: Chapters 43-44
Psalm 22

H: _____
What gentle whisper did you hear as you read today?

E: _____
How did the passages encourage you?

A: _____
How can you apply what you learned in your day today?

R: _____
What do you need to receive from God? His love, mercy, grace, comfort, or something else?

Write your favorite verse from today's reading here:

_____

_____

DAILY PRAYER

Lord, help me hear Your gentle whispers as I read Your Word. Encourage me as I learn more about Your heart. Help me apply what I learn and act according to Your will. And help me receive all You have for me to receive from You today. In Jesus' name, Amen.

DAY 23:

Matthew: Chapter 23
Acts: Chapter 23
Genesis: Chapters 45-46
Psalm 23

H: _____
What gentle whisper did you hear as you read today?

E: _____
How did the passages encourage you?

A: _____
How can you apply what you learned in your day today?

R: _____
What do you need to receive from God? His love, mercy, grace, comfort, or something else?

Write your favorite verse from today's reading here:

_____
_____

DAY 24:

Matthew: Chapter 24
Acts: Chapter 24
Genesis: Chapters 47-48
Psalm 24

H: _____
What gentle whisper did you hear as you read today?

E: _____
How did the passages encourage you?

A: _____
How can you apply what you learned in your day today?

R: _____
What do you need to receive from God? His love, mercy, grace, comfort, or something else?

Write your favorite verse from today's reading here:

_____
_____

DAILY PRAYER

Lord, help me hear Your gentle whispers as I read Your Word. Encourage me as I learn more about Your heart. Help me apply what I learn and act according to Your will. And help me receive all You have for me to receive from You today. In Jesus' name, Amen.

DAY 25:

Matthew: Chapter 25
Acts: Chapter 25
Genesis: Chapters 49-50
Psalm 25

H: _____
What gentle whisper did you hear as you read today?

E: _____
How did the passages encourage you?

A: _____
How can you apply what you learned in your day today?

R: _____
What do you need to receive from God? His love, mercy, grace, comfort, or something else?

Write your favorite verse from today's reading here:

_____

_____

DAY 26:

Matthew: Chapter 26
Acts: Chapter 26
Exodus: Chapters 1-2
Psalm 26

H: _____
What gentle whisper did you hear as you read today?

E: _____
How did the passages encourage you?

A: _____
How can you apply what you learned in your day today?

R: _____
What do you need to receive from God? His love, mercy, grace, comfort, or something else?

Write your favorite verse from today's reading here:

_____

_____

DAILY PRAYER

Lord, help me hear Your gentle whispers as I read Your Word. Encourage me as I learn more about Your heart. Help me apply what I learn and act according to Your will. And help me receive all You have for me to receive from You today. In Jesus' name, Amen.

DAY 27:

Matthew: Chapter 27
Acts: Chapter 27
Exodus: Chapters 3-4
Psalm 27

H: _____
What gentle whisper did you hear as you read today?

E: _____
How did the passages encourage you?

A: _____
How can you apply what you learned in your day today?

R: _____
What do you need to receive from God? His love, mercy, grace, comfort, or something else?

Write your favorite verse from today's reading here:

_____

_____

DAY 28:

Matthew: Chapter 28
Acts: Chapter 28
Exodus: Chapters 5-6
Psalm 28

H: _____
What gentle whisper did you hear as you read today?

E: _____
How did the passages encourage you?

A: _____
How can you apply what you learned in your day today?

R: _____
What do you need to receive from God? His love, mercy, grace, comfort, or something else?

Write your favorite verse from today's reading here:

_____

_____

DAILY PRAYER

Lord, help me hear Your gentle whispers as I read Your Word. Encourage me as I learn more about Your heart. Help me apply what I learn and act according to Your will. And help me receive all You have for me to receive from You today. In Jesus' name, Amen.

DAY 29:

Mark: Chapter 1
Romans: Chapter 1
Exodus: Chapters 7-8
Psalm 29

H: _____
What gentle whisper did you hear as you read today?

E: _____
How did the passages encourage you?

A: _____
How can you apply what you learned in your day today?

R: _____
What do you need to receive from God? His love, mercy, grace, comfort, or something else?

Write your favorite verse from today's reading here:

_____

_____

DAY 30:

Mark: Chapter 2
Romans: Chapter 2
Exodus: Chapters 9-10
Psalm 30

H: _____
What gentle whisper did you hear as you read today?

E: _____
How did the passages encourage you?

A: _____
How can you apply what you learned in your day today?

R: _____
What do you need to receive from God? His love, mercy, grace, comfort, or something else?

Write your favorite verse from today's reading here:

_____

_____

DAILY PRAYER

Lord, help me hear Your gentle whispers as I read Your Word. Encourage me as I learn more about Your heart. Help me apply what I learn and act according to Your will. And help me receive all You have for me to receive from You today. In Jesus' name, Amen.

DAY 31:

Mark: Chapter 3
Romans: Chapter 3
Exodus: Chapters 11-12
Psalm 31

H: _____
What gentle whisper did you hear as you read today?

E: _____
How did the passages encourage you?

A: _____
How can you apply what you learned in your day today?

R: _____
What do you need to receive from God? His love, mercy, grace, comfort, or something else?

Write your favorite verse from today's reading here:

_____

_____

DAY 32:

Mark: Chapter 4
Romans: Chapter 4
Exodus: Chapters 13-14
Psalm 32

H: _____
What gentle whisper did you hear as you read today?

E: _____
How did the passages encourage you?

A: _____
How can you apply what you learned in your day today?

R: _____
What do you need to receive from God? His love, mercy, grace, comfort, or something else?

Write your favorite verse from today's reading here:

_____

_____

DAILY PRAYER

Lord, help me hear Your gentle whispers as I read Your Word. Encourage me as I learn more about Your heart. Help me apply what I learn and act according to Your will. And help me receive all You have for me to receive from You today. In Jesus' name, Amen.

DAY 33:

Mark: Chapter 5
Romans: Chapter 5
Exodus: Chapters 15-16
Psalm 33

H: _____
What gentle whisper did you hear as you read today?

E: _____
How did the passages encourage you?

A: _____
How can you apply what you learned in your day today?

R: _____
What do you need to receive from God? His love, mercy, grace, comfort, or something else?

Write your favorite verse from today's reading here:

_____

_____

DAY 34:

Mark: Chapter 6
Romans: Chapter 6
Exodus: Chapters 17-18
Psalm 34

H: _____
What gentle whisper did you hear as you read today?

E: _____
How did the passages encourage you?

A: _____
How can you apply what you learned in your day today?

R: _____
What do you need to receive from God? His love, mercy, grace, comfort, or something else?

Write your favorite verse from today's reading here:

_____

_____

DAILY PRAYER

Lord, help me hear Your gentle whispers as I read Your Word. Encourage me as I learn more about Your heart. Help me apply what I learn and act according to Your will. And help me receive all You have for me to receive from You today. In Jesus' name, Amen.

DAY 35:

Mark: Chapter 7
Romans: Chapter 7
Exodus: Chapters 19-20
Psalm 35

H: _____
What gentle whisper did you hear as you read today?

E: _____
How did the passages encourage you?

A: _____
How can you apply what you learned in your day today?

R: _____
What do you need to receive from God? His love, mercy, grace, comfort, or something else?

Write your favorite verse from today's reading here:

_____
_____

DAY 36:

Mark: Chapter 8
Romans: Chapter 8
Exodus: Chapters 21-22
Psalm 36

H: _____
What gentle whisper did you hear as you read today?

E: _____
How did the passages encourage you?

A: _____
How can you apply what you learned in your day today?

R: _____
What do you need to receive from God? His love, mercy, grace, comfort, or something else?

Write your favorite verse from today's reading here:

_____
_____

DAILY PRAYER

Lord, help me hear Your gentle whispers as I read Your Word. Encourage me as I learn more about Your heart. Help me apply what I learn and act according to Your will. And help me receive all You have for me to receive from You today. In Jesus' name, Amen.

DAY 37:

Mark: Chapter 9
Romans: Chapter 9
Exodus: Chapters 23-24
Psalm 37

H: _____
What gentle whisper did you hear as you read today?

E: _____
How did the passages encourage you?

A: _____
How can you apply what you learned in your day today?

R: _____
What do you need to receive from God? His love, mercy, grace, comfort, or something else?

Write your favorite verse from today's reading here:

_____

_____

DAY 38:

Mark: Chapter 10
Romans: Chapter 10
Exodus: Chapters 25-26
Psalm 38

H: _____
What gentle whisper did you hear as you read today?

E: _____
How did the passages encourage you?

A: _____
How can you apply what you learned in your day today?

R: _____
What do you need to receive from God? His love, mercy, grace, comfort, or something else?

Write your favorite verse from today's reading here:

_____

_____

DAILY PRAYER

Lord, help me hear Your gentle whispers as I read Your Word. Encourage me as I learn more about Your heart. Help me apply what I learn and act according to Your will. And help me receive all You have for me to receive from You today. In Jesus' name, Amen.

DAY 39:

Mark: Chapter 11
Romans: Chapter 11
Exodus: Chapters 27-28
Psalm 39

H: _____
What gentle whisper did you hear as you read today?

E: _____
How did the passages encourage you?

A: _____
How can you apply what you learned in your day today?

R: _____
What do you need to receive from God? His love, mercy, grace, comfort, or something else?

Write your favorite verse from today's reading here:

_____
_____

DAY 40:

Mark: Chapter 12
Romans: Chapter 12
Exodus: Chapters 29-30
Psalm 40

H: _____
What gentle whisper did you hear as you read today?

E: _____
How did the passages encourage you?

A: _____
How can you apply what you learned in your day today?

R: _____
What do you need to receive from God? His love, mercy, grace, comfort, or something else?

Write your favorite verse from today's reading here:

_____
_____

DAILY PRAYER

Lord, help me hear Your gentle whispers as I read Your Word. Encourage me as I learn more about Your heart. Help me apply what I learn and act according to Your will. And help me receive all You have for me to receive from You today. In Jesus' name, Amen.

DAY 41:

Mark: Chapter 13
Romans: Chapter 13
Exodus: Chapters 31-32
Psalm 41

H: _____
What gentle whisper did you hear as you read today?

E: _____
How did the passages encourage you?

A: _____
How can you apply what you learned in your day today?

R: _____
What do you need to receive from God? His love, mercy, grace, comfort, or something else?

Write your favorite verse from today's reading here:

_____

_____

DAY 42:

Mark: Chapter 14
Romans: Chapter 14
Exodus: Chapters 33-34
Psalm 42

H: _____
What gentle whisper did you hear as you read today?

E: _____
How did the passages encourage you?

A: _____
How can you apply what you learned in your day today?

R: _____
What do you need to receive from God? His love, mercy, grace, comfort, or something else?

Write your favorite verse from today's reading here:

_____

_____

DAILY PRAYER

Lord, help me hear Your gentle whispers as I read Your Word. Encourage me as I learn more about Your heart. Help me apply what I learn and act according to Your will. And help me receive all You have for me to receive from You today. In Jesus' name, Amen.

DAY 43:

Mark: Chapter 15
Romans: Chapter 15
Exodus: Chapters 35-36
Psalm 43

H: _____
What gentle whisper did you hear as you read today?

E: _____
How did the passages encourage you?

A: _____
How can you apply what you learned in your day today?

R: _____
What do you need to receive from God? His love, mercy, grace, comfort, or something else?

Write your favorite verse from today's reading here:

_____

_____

DAY 44:

Mark: Chapter 16
Romans: Chapter 16
Exodus: Chapters 37-38
Psalm 44

H: _____
What gentle whisper did you hear as you read today?

E: _____
How did the passages encourage you?

A: _____
How can you apply what you learned in your day today?

R: _____
What do you need to receive from God? His love, mercy, grace, comfort, or something else?

Write your favorite verse from today's reading here:

_____

_____

DAILY PRAYER

Lord, help me hear Your gentle whispers as I read Your Word. Encourage me as I learn more about Your heart. Help me apply what I learn and act according to Your will. And help me receive all You have for me to receive from You today. In Jesus' name, Amen.

DAY 45:

Luke: Chapter 1
I Corinthians: Chapter 1
Exodus: Chapters 39-40
Psalm 45

H: _____
What gentle whisper did you hear as you read today?

E: _____
How did the passages encourage you?

A: _____
How can you apply what you learned in your day today?

R: _____
What do you need to receive from God? His love, mercy, grace, comfort, or something else?

Write your favorite verse from today's reading here:

_____

_____

DAY 46:

Luke: Chapter 2
I Corinthians: Chapter 2
Leviticus: Chapters 1-2
Psalm 46

H: _____
What gentle whisper did you hear as you read today?

E: _____
How did the passages encourage you?

A: _____
How can you apply what you learned in your day today?

R: _____
What do you need to receive from God? His love, mercy, grace, comfort, or something else?

Write your favorite verse from today's reading here:

_____

_____

DAILY PRAYER

Lord, help me hear Your gentle whispers as I read Your Word. Encourage me as I learn more about Your heart. Help me apply what I learn and act according to Your will. And help me receive all You have for me to receive from You today. In Jesus' name, Amen.

DAY 47:

Luke: Chapter 3
I Corinthians: Chapter 3
Leviticus: Chapters 3-4
Psalm 47

H: _____
What gentle whisper did you hear as you read today?

E: _____
How did the passages encourage you?

A: _____
How can you apply what you learned in your day today?

R: _____
What do you need to receive from God? His love, mercy, grace, comfort, or something else?

Write your favorite verse from today's reading here:

_____

_____

DAY 48:

Luke: Chapter 4
I Corinthians: Chapter 4
Leviticus: Chapters 5-6
Psalm 48

H: _____
What gentle whisper did you hear as you read today?

E: _____
How did the passages encourage you?

A: _____
How can you apply what you learned in your day today?

R: _____
What do you need to receive from God? His love, mercy, grace, comfort, or something else?

Write your favorite verse from today's reading here:

_____

_____

DAILY PRAYER

Lord, help me hear Your gentle whispers as I read Your Word. Encourage me as I learn more about Your heart. Help me apply what I learn and act according to Your will. And help me receive all You have for me to receive from You today. In Jesus' name, Amen.

DAY 49:

Luke: Chapter 5
I Corinthians: Chapter 5
Leviticus: Chapters 7-8
Psalm 49

H: _____
What gentle whisper did you hear as you read today?

E: _____
How did the passages encourage you?

A: _____
How can you apply what you learned in your day today?

R: _____
What do you need to receive from God? His love, mercy, grace, comfort, or something else?

Write your favorite verse from today's reading here:

_____
_____

DAY 50:

Luke: Chapter 6
I Corinthians: Chapter 6
Leviticus: Chapters 9-10
Psalm 50

H: _____
What gentle whisper did you hear as you read today?

E: _____
How did the passages encourage you?

A: _____
How can you apply what you learned in your day today?

R: _____
What do you need to receive from God? His love, mercy, grace, comfort, or something else?

Write your favorite verse from today's reading here:

_____
_____

DAILY PRAYER

Lord, help me hear Your gentle whispers as I read Your Word. Encourage me as I learn more about Your heart. Help me apply what I learn and act according to Your will. And help me receive all You have for me to receive from You today. In Jesus' name, Amen.

DAY 51:

Luke: Chapter 7
I Corinthians: Chapter 7
Leviticus: Chapters 11-12
Psalm 51

H: _____
What gentle whisper did you hear as you read today?

E: _____
How did the passages encourage you?

A: _____
How can you apply what you learned in your day today?

R: _____
What do you need to receive from God? His love, mercy, grace, comfort, or something else?

Write your favorite verse from today's reading here:

_____

_____

DAY 52:

Luke: Chapter 8
I Corinthians: Chapter 8
Leviticus: Chapters 13-14
Psalm 52

H: _____
What gentle whisper did you hear as you read today?

E: _____
How did the passages encourage you?

A: _____
How can you apply what you learned in your day today?

R: _____
What do you need to receive from God? His love, mercy, grace, comfort, or something else?

Write your favorite verse from today's reading here:

_____

_____

DAILY PRAYER

Lord, help me hear Your gentle whispers as I read Your Word. Encourage me as I learn more about Your heart. Help me apply what I learn and act according to Your will. And help me receive all You have for me to receive from You today. In Jesus' name, Amen.

DAY 53:

Luke: Chapter 9
I Corinthians: Chapter 9
Leviticus: Chapters 15-16
Psalm 53

H: _____
What gentle whisper did you hear as you read today?

E: _____
How did the passages encourage you?

A: _____
How can you apply what you learned in your day today?

R: _____
What do you need to receive from God? His love, mercy, grace, comfort, or something else?

Write your favorite verse from today's reading here:

_____

_____

DAY 54:

Luke: Chapter 10
I Corinthians: Chapter 10
Leviticus: Chapters 17-18
Psalm 54

H: _____
What gentle whisper did you hear as you read today?

E: _____
How did the passages encourage you?

A: _____
How can you apply what you learned in your day today?

R: _____
What do you need to receive from God? His love, mercy, grace, comfort, or something else?

Write your favorite verse from today's reading here:

_____

_____

DAILY PRAYER

Lord, help me hear Your gentle whispers as I read Your Word. Encourage me as I learn more about Your heart. Help me apply what I learn and act according to Your will. And help me receive all You have for me to receive from You today. In Jesus' name, Amen.

DAY 55: FEB 24

Luke: Chapter 11
I Corinthians: Chapter 11
Leviticus: Chapters 19-20
Psalm 55

H: _____
What gentle whisper did you hear as you read today?

E: _____
How did the passages encourage you?

A: _____
How can you apply what you learned in your day today?

R: _____
What do you need to receive from God? His love, mercy, grace, comfort, or something else?

Write your favorite verse from today's reading here:

_____
_____

DAY 56: FEB 25

Luke: Chapter 12
I Corinthians: Chapter 12
Leviticus: Chapters 21-22
Psalm 56

H: _____
What gentle whisper did you hear as you read today?

E: _____
How did the passages encourage you?

A: _____
How can you apply what you learned in your day today?

R: _____
What do you need to receive from God? His love, mercy, grace, comfort, or something else?

Write your favorite verse from today's reading here:

_____
_____

DAILY PRAYER

Lord, help me hear Your gentle whispers as I read Your Word. Encourage me as I learn more about Your heart. Help me apply what I learn and act according to Your will. And help me receive all You have for me to receive from You today. In Jesus' name, Amen.

DAY 57: FEB 26

Luke: Chapter 13
I Corinthians: Chapter 13
Leviticus: Chapters 23-24
Psalm 57

H: _____
What gentle whisper did you hear as you read today?

E: _____
How did the passages encourage you?

A: _____
How can you apply what you learned in your day today?

R: _____
What do you need to receive from God? His love, mercy, grace, comfort, or something else?

Write your favorite verse from today's reading here:

_____
_____

DAY 58: FEB 27

Luke: Chapter 14
I Corinthians: Chapter 14
Leviticus: Chapters 25-27
Psalm 58

H: _____
What gentle whisper did you hear as you read today?

E: _____
How did the passages encourage you?

A: _____
How can you apply what you learned in your day today?

R: _____
What do you need to receive from God? His love, mercy, grace, comfort, or something else?

Write your favorite verse from today's reading here:

_____
_____

DAILY PRAYER

Lord, help me hear Your gentle whispers as I read Your Word. Encourage me as I learn more about Your heart. Help me apply what I learn and act according to Your will. And help me receive all You have for me to receive from You today. In Jesus' name, Amen.

DAY 59:   FEB 28

Luke: Chapter 15
I Corinthians: Chapter 15
Numbers: Chapters 1-2
Psalm 59

H: _____
What gentle whisper did you hear as you read today?

E: _____
How did the passages encourage you?

A: _____
How can you apply what you learned in your day today?

R: _____
What do you need to receive from God? His love, mercy, grace, comfort, or something else?

Write your favorite verse from today's reading here:

_____

_____

DAY 60:   MARCH 1

Luke: Chapter 16
I Corinthians: Chapter 16
Numbers: Chapters 3-4
Psalm 60

H: _____
What gentle whisper did you hear as you read today?

E: _____
How did the passages encourage you?

A: _____
How can you apply what you learned in your day today?

R: _____
What do you need to receive from God? His love, mercy, grace, comfort, or something else?

Write your favorite verse from today's reading here:

_____

_____

DAILY PRAYER

Lord, help me hear Your gentle whispers as I read Your Word. Encourage me as I learn more about Your heart. Help me apply what I learn and act according to Your will. And help me receive all You have for me to receive from You today. In Jesus' name, Amen.

DAY 61: MARCH 2

Luke: Chapter 17
II Corinthians: Chapter 1
Numbers: Chapters 5-6
Psalm 61

H: _____
What gentle whisper did you hear as you read today?

E: _____
How did the passages encourage you?

A: _____
How can you apply what you learned in your day today?

R: _____
What do you need to receive from God? His love, mercy, grace, comfort, or something else?

Write your favorite verse from today's reading here:

_____

_____

DAY 62: MARCH 3

Luke: Chapter 18
II Corinthians: Chapter 2
Numbers: Chapters 7-8
Psalm 62

H: _____
What gentle whisper did you hear as you read today?

E: _____
How did the passages encourage you?

A: _____
How can you apply what you learned in your day today?

R: _____
What do you need to receive from God? His love, mercy, grace, comfort, or something else?

Write your favorite verse from today's reading here:

_____

_____

DAILY PRAYER

Lord, help me hear Your gentle whispers as I read Your Word. Encourage me as I learn more about Your heart. Help me apply what I learn and act according to Your will. And help me receive all You have for me to receive from You today. In Jesus' name, Amen.

DAY 63: MAR 4

Luke: Chapter 19
II Corinthians: Chapter 3
Numbers: Chapters 9-10
Psalm 63

H: _____
What gentle whisper did you hear as you read today?

E: _____
How did the passages encourage you?

A: _____
How can you apply what you learned in your day today?

R: _____
What do you need to receive from God? His love, mercy, grace, comfort, or something else?

Write your favorite verse from today's reading here:

_____
_____

DAY 64: MAR 5

Luke: Chapter 20
II Corinthians: Chapter 4
Numbers: Chapters 11-12
Psalm 64

H: _____
What gentle whisper did you hear as you read today?

E: _____
How did the passages encourage you?

A: _____
How can you apply what you learned in your day today?

R: _____
What do you need to receive from God? His love, mercy, grace, comfort, or something else?

Write your favorite verse from today's reading here:

_____
_____

DAILY PRAYER

Lord, help me hear Your gentle whispers as I read Your Word. Encourage me as I learn more about Your heart. Help me apply what I learn and act according to Your will. And help me receive all You have for me to receive from You today. In Jesus' name, Amen.

DAY 65: MARCH 6

Luke: Chapter 21
II Corinthians: Chapter 5
Numbers: Chapters 13-14
Psalm 65

H: _____
What gentle whisper did you hear as you read today?

E: _____
How did the passages encourage you?

A: _____
How can you apply what you learned in your day today?

R: _____
What do you need to receive from God? His love, mercy, grace, comfort, or something else?

Write your favorite verse from today's reading here:

_____

_____

DAY 66: MARCH 7

Luke: Chapter 22
II Corinthians: Chapter 6
Numbers: Chapters 15-16
Psalm 66

H: _____
What gentle whisper did you hear as you read today?

E: _____
How did the passages encourage you?

A: _____
How can you apply what you learned in your day today?

R: _____
What do you need to receive from God? His love, mercy, grace, comfort, or something else?

Write your favorite verse from today's reading here:

_____

_____

DAILY PRAYER

Lord, help me hear Your gentle whispers as I read Your Word. Encourage me as I learn more about Your heart. Help me apply what I learn and act according to Your will. And help me receive all You have for me to receive from You today. In Jesus' name, Amen.

DAY 67 MARCH 8

Luke: Chapter 23
II Corinthians: Chapter 7
Numbers: Chapters 17-18
Psalm 67

H: _____
What gentle whisper did you hear as you read today?

E: _____
How did the passages encourage you?

A: _____
How can you apply what you learned in your day today?

R: _____
What do you need to receive from God? His love, mercy, grace, comfort, or something else?

Write your favorite verse from today's reading here:

_____

_____

DAY 68: MARCH 9

Luke: Chapter 24
II Corinthians: Chapter 8
Numbers: Chapters 19-20
Psalm 68

H: _____
What gentle whisper did you hear as you read today?

E: _____
How did the passages encourage you?

A: _____
How can you apply what you learned in your day today?

R: _____
What do you need to receive from God? His love, mercy, grace, comfort, or something else?

Write your favorite verse from today's reading here:

_____

_____

DAILY PRAYER

Lord, help me hear Your gentle whispers as I read Your Word. Encourage me as I learn more about Your heart. Help me apply what I learn and act according to Your will. And help me receive all You have for me to receive from You today. In Jesus' name, Amen.

DAY 69: MARCH 10

John: Chapter 1
II Corinthians: Chapter 9
Numbers: Chapters 21-22
Psalm 69

H: _____
What gentle whisper did you hear as you read today?

E: _____
How did the passages encourage you?

A: _____
How can you apply what you learned in your day today?

R: _____
What do you need to receive from God? His love, mercy, grace, comfort, or something else?

Write your favorite verse from today's reading here:

_____

DAY 70: MARCH 11

John: Chapter 2
II Corinthians: Chapter 10
Numbers: Chapters 23-24
Psalm 70

H: _____
What gentle whisper did you hear as you read today?

E: _____
How did the passages encourage you?

A: _____
How can you apply what you learned in your day today?

R: _____
What do you need to receive from God? His love, mercy, grace, comfort, or something else?

Write your favorite verse from today's reading here:

_____

DAILY PRAYER

Lord, help me hear Your gentle whispers as I read Your Word. Encourage me as I learn more about Your heart. Help me apply what I learn and act according to Your will. And help me receive all You have for me to receive from You today. In Jesus' name, Amen.

DAY 71: MARCH 12

John: Chapter 3
II Corinthians: Chapter 11
Numbers: Chapters 25-26
Psalm 71

H: _____
What gentle whisper did you hear as you read today?

E: _____
How did the passages encourage you?

A: _____
How can you apply what you learned in your day today?

R: _____
What do you need to receive from God? His love, mercy, grace, comfort, or something else?

Write your favorite verse from today's reading here:

_____
_____

DAY 72: MARCH 13

John: Chapter 4
II Corinthians: Chapter 12
Numbers: Chapters 27-28
Psalm 72

H: _____
What gentle whisper did you hear as you read today?

E: _____
How did the passages encourage you?

A: _____
How can you apply what you learned in your day today?

R: _____
What do you need to receive from God? His love, mercy, grace, comfort, or something else?

Write your favorite verse from today's reading here:

_____
_____

DAILY PRAYER

Lord, help me hear Your gentle whispers as I read Your Word. Encourage me as I learn more about Your heart. Help me apply what I learn and act according to Your will. And help me receive all You have for me to receive from You today. In Jesus' name, Amen.

DAY 73: MARCH 14

John: Chapter 5
II Corinthians: Chapter 13
Numbers: Chapters 29-30
Psalm 73

H: _____
What gentle whisper did you hear as you read today?

E: _____
How did the passages encourage you?

A: _____
How can you apply what you learned in your day today?

R: _____
What do you need to receive from God? His love, mercy, grace, comfort, or something else?

Write your favorite verse from today's reading here:

_____
_____

DAY 74: MARCH 15

John: Chapter 6
Galatians: Chapter 1
Numbers: Chapters 31-32
Psalm 74

H: _____
What gentle whisper did you hear as you read today?

E: _____
How did the passages encourage you?

A: _____
How can you apply what you learned in your day today?

R: _____
What do you need to receive from God? His love, mercy, grace, comfort, or something else?

Write your favorite verse from today's reading here:

_____
_____

DAILY PRAYER

Lord, help me hear Your gentle whispers as I read Your Word. Encourage me as I learn more about Your heart. Help me apply what I learn and act according to Your will. And help me receive all You have for me to receive from You today. In Jesus' name, Amen.

DAY 75: MARCH 16

John: Chapter 7
Galatians: Chapter 2
Numbers: Chapters 33-34
Psalm 75

H: _____
What gentle whisper did you hear as you read today?

E: _____
How did the passages encourage you?

A: _____
How can you apply what you learned in your day today?

R: _____
What do you need to receive from God? His love, mercy, grace, comfort, or something else?

Write your favorite verse from today's reading here:

_____

_____

DAY 76: MARCH 17

John: Chapter 8
Galatians: Chapter 3
Numbers: Chapters 35-36
Psalm 76

H: _____
What gentle whisper did you hear as you read today?

E: _____
How did the passages encourage you?

A: _____
How can you apply what you learned in your day today?

R: _____
What do you need to receive from God? His love, mercy, grace, comfort, or something else?

Write your favorite verse from today's reading here:

_____

_____

DAILY PRAYER

Lord, help me hear Your gentle whispers as I read Your Word. Encourage me as I learn more about Your heart. Help me apply what I learn and act according to Your will. And help me receive all You have for me to receive from You today. In Jesus' name, Amen.

DAY 77: MARCH 18

John: Chapter 9
Galatians: Chapter 4
Deuteronomy: Chapters 1-2
Psalm 77

H: _____
What gentle whisper did you hear as you read today?

E: _____
How did the passages encourage you?

A: _____
How can you apply what you learned in your day today?

R: _____
What do you need to receive from God? His love, mercy, grace, comfort, or something else?

Write your favorite verse from today's reading here:

_____

_____

DAY 78: MARCH 19

John: Chapter 10
Galatians: Chapter 5
Deuteronomy: Chapters 3-4
Psalm 78

H: _____
What gentle whisper did you hear as you read today?

E: _____
How did the passages encourage you?

A: _____
How can you apply what you learned in your day today?

R: _____
What do you need to receive from God? His love, mercy, grace, comfort, or something else?

Write your favorite verse from today's reading here:

_____

_____

DAILY PRAYER

Lord, help me hear Your gentle whispers as I read Your Word. Encourage me as I learn more about Your heart. Help me apply what I learn and act according to Your will. And help me receive all You have for me to receive from You today. In Jesus' name, Amen.

DAY 79: MARCH 20

John: Chapter 11
Galatians: Chapter 6
Deuteronomy: Chapters 5-6
Psalm 79

H: _____
What gentle whisper did you hear as you read today?

E: _____
How did the passages encourage you?

A: _____
How can you apply what you learned in your day today?

R: _____
What do you need to receive from God? His love, mercy, grace, comfort, or something else?

Write your favorite verse from today's reading here:

_____
_____

DAY 80: MARCH 21

John: Chapter 12
Ephesians: Chapter 1
Deuteronomy: Chapters 7-8
Psalm 80

H: _____
What gentle whisper did you hear as you read today?

E: _____
How did the passages encourage you?

A: _____
How can you apply what you learned in your day today?

R: _____
What do you need to receive from God? His love, mercy, grace, comfort, or something else?

Write your favorite verse from today's reading here:

_____
_____

DAILY PRAYER

Lord, help me hear Your gentle whispers as I read Your Word. Encourage me as I learn more about Your heart. Help me apply what I learn and act according to Your will. And help me receive all You have for me to receive from You today. In Jesus' name, Amen.

DAY 81: MARCH 22

John: Chapter 13
Ephesians: Chapter 2
Deuteronomy: Chapters 9-10
Psalm 81

H: _____
What gentle whisper did you hear as you read today?

E: _____
How did the passages encourage you?

A: _____
How can you apply what you learned in your day today?

R: _____
What do you need to receive from God? His love, mercy, grace, comfort, or something else?

Write your favorite verse from today's reading here:

_____

DAY 82: MARCH 23

John: Chapter 14
Ephesians: Chapter 3
Deuteronomy: Chapters 11-12
Psalm 82

H: _____
What gentle whisper did you hear as you read today?

E: _____
How did the passages encourage you?

A: _____
How can you apply what you learned in your day today?

R: _____
What do you need to receive from God? His love, mercy, grace, comfort, or something else?

Write your favorite verse from today's reading here:

_____

DAILY PRAYER

Lord, help me hear Your gentle whispers as I read Your Word. Encourage me as I learn more about Your heart. Help me apply what I learn and act according to Your will. And help me receive all You have for me to receive from You today. In Jesus' name, Amen.

DAY 83: MARCH 24

John: Chapter 15
Ephesians: Chapter 4
Deuteronomy: Chapters 13-14
Psalm 83

H: _____
What gentle whisper did you hear as you read today?

E: _____
How did the passages encourage you?

A: _____
How can you apply what you learned in your day today?

R: _____
What do you need to receive from God? His love, mercy, grace, comfort, or something else?

Write your favorite verse from today's reading here:

_____
_____

DAY 84: MARCH 25

John: Chapter 16
Ephesians: Chapter 5
Deuteronomy: Chapters 15-16
Psalm 84

H: _____
What gentle whisper did you hear as you read today?

E: _____
How did the passages encourage you?

A: _____
How can you apply what you learned in your day today?

R: _____
What do you need to receive from God? His love, mercy, grace, comfort, or something else?

Write your favorite verse from today's reading here:

_____
_____

DAILY PRAYER

Lord, help me hear Your gentle whispers as I read Your Word. Encourage me as I learn more about Your heart. Help me apply what I learn and act according to Your will. And help me receive all You have for me to receive from You today. In Jesus' name, Amen.

DAY 85: MARCH 26

John: Chapter 17
Ephesians: Chapter 6
Deuteronomy: Chapters 17-18
Psalm 85

H: _____
What gentle whisper did you hear as you read today?

E: _____
How did the passages encourage you?

A: _____
How can you apply what you learned in your day today?

R: _____
What do you need to receive from God? His love, mercy, grace, comfort, or something else?

Write your favorite verse from today's reading here:

_____

_____

DAY 86: MARCH 27

John: Chapter 18
Philippians: Chapter 1
Deuteronomy: Chapters 19-20
Psalm 86

H: _____
What gentle whisper did you hear as you read today?

E: _____
How did the passages encourage you?

A: _____
How can you apply what you learned in your day today?

R: _____
What do you need to receive from God? His love, mercy, grace, comfort, or something else?

Write your favorite verse from today's reading here:

_____

_____

DAILY PRAYER

Lord, help me hear Your gentle whispers as I read Your Word. Encourage me as I learn more about Your heart. Help me apply what I learn and act according to Your will. And help me receive all You have for me to receive from You today. In Jesus' name, Amen.

DAY 87: MARCH 28

John: Chapter 19
Philippians: Chapter 2
Deuteronomy: Chapters 21-22
Psalm 87

H: _____
What gentle whisper did you hear as you read today?

E: _____
How did the passages encourage you?

A: _____
How can you apply what you learned in your day today?

R: _____
What do you need to receive from God? His love, mercy, grace, comfort, or something else?

Write your favorite verse from today's reading here:

_____

_____

DAY 88: MARCH 29

John: Chapter 20
Philippians: Chapter 3
Deuteronomy: Chapters 23-24
Psalm 88

H: _____
What gentle whisper did you hear as you read today?

E: _____
How did the passages encourage you?

A: _____
How can you apply what you learned in your day today?

R: _____
What do you need to receive from God? His love, mercy, grace, comfort, or something else?

Write your favorite verse from today's reading here:

_____

_____

DAILY PRAYER

Lord, help me hear Your gentle whispers as I read Your Word. Encourage me as I learn more about Your heart. Help me apply what I learn and act according to Your will. And help me receive all You have for me to receive from You today. In Jesus' name, Amen.

DAY 89: MARCH 30

John: Chapter 21
Philippians: Chapter 4
Deuteronomy: Chapters 25-26
Psalm 89

H: _____
What gentle whisper did you hear as you read today?

E: _____
How did the passages encourage you?

A: _____
How can you apply what you learned in your day today?

R: _____
What do you need to receive from God? His love, mercy, grace, comfort, or something else?

Write your favorite verse from today's reading here:

_____
_____

DAY 90: MARCH 31

Matthew: Chapter 1
Colossians: Chapter 1
Deuteronomy: Chapters 27-28
Psalm 90

H: _____
What gentle whisper did you hear as you read today?

E: _____
How did the passages encourage you?

A: _____
How can you apply what you learned in your day today?

R: _____
What do you need to receive from God? His love, mercy, grace, comfort, or something else?

Write your favorite verse from today's reading here:

_____
_____

DAILY PRAYER

Lord, help me hear Your gentle whispers as I read Your Word. Encourage me as I learn more about Your heart. Help me apply what I learn and act according to Your will. And help me receive all You have for me to receive from You today. In Jesus' name, Amen.

DAY 91: APRIL 1

Matthew: Chapter 2
Colossians: Chapter 2
Deuteronomy: Chapters 29-30
Psalm 91

H: _____
What gentle whisper did you hear as you read today?

E: _____
How did the passages encourage you?

A: _____
How can you apply what you learned in your day today?

R: _____
What do you need to receive from God? His love, mercy, grace, comfort, or something else?

Write your favorite verse from today's reading here:

_____

_____

DAY 92: APRIL 2

Matthew: Chapter 3
Colossians: Chapter 3
Deuteronomy: Chapters 31-32
Psalm 92

H: _____
What gentle whisper did you hear as you read today?

E: _____
How did the passages encourage you?

A: _____
How can you apply what you learned in your day today?

R: _____
What do you need to receive from God? His love, mercy, grace, comfort, or something else?

Write your favorite verse from today's reading here:

_____

_____

DAILY PRAYER

Lord, help me hear Your gentle whispers as I read Your Word. Encourage me as I learn more about Your heart. Help me apply what I learn and act according to Your will. And help me receive all You have for me to receive from You today. In Jesus' name, Amen.

DAY 93:   APRIL 3

Matthew: Chapter 4
Colossians: Chapter 4
Deuteronomy: Chapters 33-34
Psalm 93

H: _____
What gentle whisper did you hear as you read today?

E: _____
How did the passages encourage you?

A: _____
How can you apply what you learned in your day today?

R: _____
What do you need to receive from God? His love, mercy, grace, comfort, or something else?

Write your favorite verse from today's reading here:

_____

_____

DAY 94:

Matthew: Chapter 5
I Thessalonians: Chapter 1
Joshua: Chapters 1-2
Psalm 94

H: _____
What gentle whisper did you hear as you read today?

E: _____
How did the passages encourage you?

A: _____
How can you apply what you learned in your day today?

R: _____
What do you need to receive from God? His love, mercy, grace, comfort, or something else?

Write your favorite verse from today's reading here:

_____

_____

DAILY PRAYER

Lord, help me hear Your gentle whispers as I read Your Word. Encourage me as I learn more about Your heart. Help me apply what I learn and act according to Your will. And help me receive all You have for me to receive from You today. In Jesus' name, Amen.

DAY 95:

Matthew: Chapter 6
I Thessalonians: Chapter 2
Joshua: Chapters 3-4
Psalm 95

H: _____
What gentle whisper did you hear as you read today?

E: _____
How did the passages encourage you?

A: _____
How can you apply what you learned in your day today?

R: _____
What do you need to receive from God? His love, mercy, grace, comfort, or something else?

Write your favorite verse from today's reading here:

_____

_____

DAY 96:

Matthew: Chapter 7
I Thessalonians: Chapter 3
Joshua: Chapters 5-6
Psalm 96

H: _____
What gentle whisper did you hear as you read today?

E: _____
How did the passages encourage you?

A: _____
How can you apply what you learned in your day today?

R: _____
What do you need to receive from God? His love, mercy, grace, comfort, or something else?

Write your favorite verse from today's reading here:

_____

_____

DAILY PRAYER

Lord, help me hear Your gentle whispers as I read Your Word. Encourage me as I learn more about Your heart. Help me apply what I learn and act according to Your will. And help me receive all You have for me to receive from You today. In Jesus' name, Amen.

DAY 97:

Matthew: Chapter 8
I Thessalonians: Chapter 4
Joshua: Chapters 7-8
Psalm 97

H: _____
What gentle whisper did you hear as you read today?

E: _____
How did the passages encourage you?

A: _____
How can you apply what you learned in your day today?

R: _____
What do you need to receive from God? His love, mercy, grace, comfort, or something else?

Write your favorite verse from today's reading here:

_____

_____

DAY 98:

Matthew: Chapter 9
I Thessalonians: Chapter 5
Joshua: Chapters 9-10
Psalm 98

H: _____
What gentle whisper did you hear as you read today?

E: _____
How did the passages encourage you?

A: _____
How can you apply what you learned in your day today?

R: _____
What do you need to receive from God? His love, mercy, grace, comfort, or something else?

Write your favorite verse from today's reading here:

_____

_____

DAILY PRAYER

Lord, help me hear Your gentle whispers as I read Your Word. Encourage me as I learn more about Your heart. Help me apply what I learn and act according to Your will. And help me receive all You have for me to receive from You today. In Jesus' name, Amen.

DAY 99:

Matthew: Chapter 10
II Thessalonians: Chapter 1
Joshua: Chapters 11-12
Psalm 99

H: _____
What gentle whisper did you hear as you read today?

E: _____
How did the passages encourage you?

A: _____
How can you apply what you learned in your day today?

R: _____
What do you need to receive from God? His love, mercy, grace, comfort, or something else?

Write your favorite verse from today's reading here:

_____

_____

DAY 100:

Matthew: Chapter 11
II Thessalonians: Chapter 2
Joshua: Chapters 13-14
Psalm 100

H: _____
What gentle whisper did you hear as you read today?

E: _____
How did the passages encourage you?

A: _____
How can you apply what you learned in your day today?

R: _____
What do you need to receive from God? His love, mercy, grace, comfort, or something else?

Write your favorite verse from today's reading here:

_____

_____

DAILY PRAYER

Lord, help me hear Your gentle whispers as I read Your Word. Encourage me as I learn more about Your heart. Help me apply what I learn and act according to Your will. And help me receive all You have for me to receive from You today. In Jesus' name, Amen.

DAY 101:

Matthew: Chapter 12
II Thessalonians: Chapter 3
Joshua: Chapters 15-16
Psalm 101

H: _____
What gentle whisper did you hear as you read today?

E: _____
How did the passages encourage you?

A: _____
How can you apply what you learned in your day today?

R: _____
What do you need to receive from God? His love, mercy, grace, comfort, or something else?

Write your favorite verse from today's reading here:

_____

_____

DAY 102:

Matthew: Chapter 13
I Timothy: Chapter 1
Joshua: Chapters 17-18
Psalm 102

H: _____
What gentle whisper did you hear as you read today?

E: _____
How did the passages encourage you?

A: _____
How can you apply what you learned in your day today?

R: _____
What do you need to receive from God? His love, mercy, grace, comfort, or something else?

Write your favorite verse from today's reading here:

_____

_____

DAILY PRAYER

Lord, help me hear Your gentle whispers as I read Your Word. Encourage me as I learn more about Your heart. Help me apply what I learn and act according to Your will. And help me receive all You have for me to receive from You today. In Jesus' name, Amen.

DAY 103:

Matthew: Chapter 14
I Timothy: Chapter 2
Joshua: Chapters 19-20
Psalm 103

H: _____
What gentle whisper did you hear as you read today?

E: _____
How did the passages encourage you?

A: _____
How can you apply what you learned in your day today?

R: _____
What do you need to receive from God? His love, mercy, grace, comfort, or something else?

Write your favorite verse from today's reading here:

_____
_____

DAY 104:

Matthew: Chapter 15
I Timothy: Chapter 3
Joshua: Chapters 21-22
Psalm 104

H: _____
What gentle whisper did you hear as you read today?

E: _____
How did the passages encourage you?

A: _____
How can you apply what you learned in your day today?

R: _____
What do you need to receive from God? His love, mercy, grace, comfort, or something else?

Write your favorite verse from today's reading here:

_____
_____

DAILY PRAYER

Lord, help me hear Your gentle whispers as I read Your Word. Encourage me as I learn more about Your heart. Help me apply what I learn and act according to Your will. And help me receive all You have for me to receive from You today. In Jesus' name, Amen.

DAY 105:

Matthew: Chapter 16
I Timothy: Chapter 4
Joshua: Chapters 23-24
Psalm 105

H: _____
What gentle whisper did you hear as you read today?

E: _____
How did the passages encourage you?

A: _____
How can you apply what you learned in your day today?

R: _____
What do you need to receive from God? His love, mercy, grace, comfort, or something else?

Write your favorite verse from today's reading here:

_____
_____

DAY 106:

Matthew: Chapter 17
I Timothy: Chapter 5
Judges: Chapters 1-2
Psalm 106

H: _____
What gentle whisper did you hear as you read today?

E: _____
How did the passages encourage you?

A: _____
How can you apply what you learned in your day today?

R: _____
What do you need to receive from God? His love, mercy, grace, comfort, or something else?

Write your favorite verse from today's reading here:

_____
_____

DAILY PRAYER

Lord, help me hear Your gentle whispers as I read Your Word. Encourage me as I learn more about Your heart. Help me apply what I learn and act according to Your will. And help me receive all You have for me to receive from You today. In Jesus' name, Amen.

DAY 107:

Matthew: Chapter 18
I Timothy: Chapter 6
Judges: Chapters 3-4
Psalm 107

H: _____
What gentle whisper did you hear as you read today?

E: _____
How did the passages encourage you?

A: _____
How can you apply what you learned in your day today?

R: _____
What do you need to receive from God? His love, mercy, grace, comfort, or something else?

Write your favorite verse from today's reading here:

_____

_____

DAY 108:

Matthew: Chapter 19
II Timothy: Chapter 1
Judges: Chapters 5-6
Psalm 108

H: _____
What gentle whisper did you hear as you read today?

E: _____
How did the passages encourage you?

A: _____
How can you apply what you learned in your day today?

R: _____
What do you need to receive from God? His love, mercy, grace, comfort, or something else?

Write your favorite verse from today's reading here:

_____

_____

DAILY PRAYER

Lord, help me hear Your gentle whispers as I read Your Word. Encourage me as I learn more about Your heart. Help me apply what I learn and act according to Your will. And help me receive all You have for me to receive from You today. In Jesus' name, Amen.

DAY 109:

Matthew: Chapter 20
II Timothy: Chapter 2
Judges: Chapters 7-8
Psalm 109

H: _____
What gentle whisper did you hear as you read today?

E: _____
How did the passages encourage you?

A: _____
How can you apply what you learned in your day today?

R: _____
What do you need to receive from God? His love, mercy, grace, comfort, or something else?

Write your favorite verse from today's reading here:

_____

_____

DAY 110:

Matthew: Chapter 21
II Timothy: Chapter 3
Judges: Chapters 9-10
Psalm 110

H: _____
What gentle whisper did you hear as you read today?

E: _____
How did the passages encourage you?

A: _____
How can you apply what you learned in your day today?

R: _____
What do you need to receive from God? His love, mercy, grace, comfort, or something else?

Write your favorite verse from today's reading here:

_____

_____

DAILY PRAYER

Lord, help me hear Your gentle whispers as I read Your Word. Encourage me as I learn more about Your heart. Help me apply what I learn and act according to Your will. And help me receive all You have for me to receive from You today. In Jesus' name, Amen.

DAY 111:

Matthew: Chapter 22
II Timothy: Chapter 4
Judges: Chapters 11-12
Psalm 111

H: _____
What gentle whisper did you hear as you read today?

E: _____
How did the passages encourage you?

A: _____
How can you apply what you learned in your day today?

R: _____
What do you need to receive from God? His love, mercy, grace, comfort, or something else?

Write your favorite verse from today's reading here:

_____

_____

DAY 112:

Matthew: Chapter 23
Titus: Chapter 1
Judges: Chapters 13-14
Psalm 112

H: _____
What gentle whisper did you hear as you read today?

E: _____
How did the passages encourage you?

A: _____
How can you apply what you learned in your day today?

R: _____
What do you need to receive from God? His love, mercy, grace, comfort, or something else?

Write your favorite verse from today's reading here:

_____

_____

DAILY PRAYER

Lord, help me hear Your gentle whispers as I read Your Word. Encourage me as I learn more about Your heart. Help me apply what I learn and act according to Your will. And help me receive all You have for me to receive from You today. In Jesus' name, Amen.

DAY 113:

Matthew: Chapter 24
Titus: Chapter 2
Judges: Chapters 15-16
Psalm 113

H: _____
What gentle whisper did you hear as you read today?

E: _____
How did the passages encourage you?

A: _____
How can you apply what you learned in your day today?

R: _____
What do you need to receive from God? His love, mercy, grace, comfort, or something else?

Write your favorite verse from today's reading here:

_____

_____

DAY 114:

Matthew: Chapter 25
Titus: Chapter 3
Judges: Chapters 17-18
Psalm 114

H: _____
What gentle whisper did you hear as you read today?

E: _____
How did the passages encourage you?

A: _____
How can you apply what you learned in your day today?

R: _____
What do you need to receive from God? His love, mercy, grace, comfort, or something else?

Write your favorite verse from today's reading here:

_____

_____

DAILY PRAYER

Lord, help me hear Your gentle whispers as I read Your Word. Encourage me as I learn more about Your heart. Help me apply what I learn and act according to Your will. And help me receive all You have for me to receive from You today. In Jesus' name, Amen.

DAY 115:

Matthew: Chapter 26
Philemon: Chapter 1
Judges: Chapters 19-21
Psalm 115

H: _____
What gentle whisper did you hear as you read today?

E: _____
How did the passages encourage you?

A: _____
How can you apply what you learned in your day today?

R: _____
What do you need to receive from God? His love, mercy, grace, comfort, or something else?

Write your favorite verse from today's reading here:

_____

_____

DAY 116:

Matthew: Chapter 27
Hebrews: Chapter 1
Ruth: Chapter 1-4
Psalm 116

H: _____
What gentle whisper did you hear as you read today?

E: _____
How did the passages encourage you?

A: _____
How can you apply what you learned in your day today?

R: _____
What do you need to receive from God? His love, mercy, grace, comfort, or something else?

Write your favorite verse from today's reading here:

_____

_____

DAILY PRAYER

Lord, help me hear Your gentle whispers as I read Your Word. Encourage me as I learn more about Your heart. Help me apply what I learn and act according to Your will. And help me receive all You have for me to receive from You today. In Jesus' name, Amen.

DAY 117:

Matthew: Chapter 28
Hebrews: Chapter 2
I Samuel: Chapters 1-2
Psalm 117

H: _____
What gentle whisper did you hear as you read today?

E: _____
How did the passages encourage you?

A: _____
How can you apply what you learned in your day today?

R: _____
What do you need to receive from God? His love, mercy, grace, comfort, or something else?

Write your favorite verse from today's reading here:

_____

_____

DAY 118:

Mark: Chapter 1
Hebrews: Chapter 3
I Samuel: Chapters 3-4
Psalm 118

H: _____
What gentle whisper did you hear as you read today?

E: _____
How did the passages encourage you?

A: _____
How can you apply what you learned in your day today?

R: _____
What do you need to receive from God? His love, mercy, grace, comfort, or something else?

Write your favorite verse from today's reading here:

_____

_____

DAILY PRAYER

Lord, help me hear Your gentle whispers as I read Your Word. Encourage me as I learn more about Your heart. Help me apply what I learn and act according to Your will. And help me receive all You have for me to receive from You today. In Jesus' name, Amen.

DAY 119:

Mark: Chapter 2
Hebrews: Chapter 4
I Samuel: Chapters 5-6
Psalm 119

H: _____
What gentle whisper did you hear as you read today?

E: _____
How did the passages encourage you?

A: _____
How can you apply what you learned in your day today?

R: _____
What do you need to receive from God? His love, mercy, grace, comfort, or something else?

Write your favorite verse from today's reading here:

_____
_____

DAY 120:

Mark: Chapter 3
Hebrews: Chapter 5
I Samuel: Chapters 7-8
Psalm 120

H: _____
What gentle whisper did you hear as you read today?

E: _____
How did the passages encourage you?

A: _____
How can you apply what you learned in your day today?

R: _____
What do you need to receive from God? His love, mercy, grace, comfort, or something else?

Write your favorite verse from today's reading here:

_____
_____

DAILY PRAYER

Lord, help me hear Your gentle whispers as I read Your Word. Encourage me as I learn more about Your heart. Help me apply what I learn and act according to Your will. And help me receive all You have for me to receive from You today. In Jesus' name, Amen.

DAY 121:

Mark: Chapter 4
Hebrews: Chapter 6
I Samuel: Chapters 9-10
Psalm 121

H: _____
What gentle whisper did you hear as you read today?

E: _____
How did the passages encourage you?

A: _____
How can you apply what you learned in your day today?

R: _____
What do you need to receive from God? His love, mercy, grace, comfort, or something else?

Write your favorite verse from today's reading here:

_____

_____

DAY 122:

Mark: Chapter 5
Hebrews: Chapter 7
I Samuel: Chapters 11-12
Psalm 122

H: _____
What gentle whisper did you hear as you read today?

E: _____
How did the passages encourage you?

A: _____
How can you apply what you learned in your day today?

R: _____
What do you need to receive from God? His love, mercy, grace, comfort, or something else?

Write your favorite verse from today's reading here:

_____

_____

DAILY PRAYER

Lord, help me hear Your gentle whispers as I read Your Word. Encourage me as I learn more about Your heart. Help me apply what I learn and act according to Your will. And help me receive all You have for me to receive from You today. In Jesus' name, Amen.

DAY 123:

Mark: Chapter 6
Hebrews: Chapter 8
I Samuel: Chapters 13-14
Psalm 123

H: _____
What gentle whisper did you hear as you read today?

E: _____
How did the passages encourage you?

A: _____
How can you apply what you learned in your day today?

R: _____
What do you need to receive from God? His love, mercy, grace, comfort, or something else?

Write your favorite verse from today's reading here:

_____

_____

DAY 124:

Mark: Chapter 7
Hebrews: Chapter 9
I Samuel: Chapters 15-16
Psalm 124

H: _____
What gentle whisper did you hear as you read today?

E: _____
How did the passages encourage you?

A: _____
How can you apply what you learned in your day today?

R: _____
What do you need to receive from God? His love, mercy, grace, comfort, or something else?

Write your favorite verse from today's reading here:

_____

_____

DAILY PRAYER

Lord, help me hear Your gentle whispers as I read Your Word. Encourage me as I learn more about Your heart. Help me apply what I learn and act according to Your will. And help me receive all You have for me to receive from You today. In Jesus' name, Amen.

DAY 125:

Mark: Chapter 8
Hebrews: Chapter 10
I Samuel: Chapters 17-18
Psalm 125

H: _____
What gentle whisper did you hear as you read today?

E: _____
How did the passages encourage you?

A: _____
How can you apply what you learned in your day today?

R: _____
What do you need to receive from God? His love, mercy, grace, comfort, or something else?

Write your favorite verse from today's reading here:

_____

_____

DAY 126:

Mark: Chapter 9
Hebrews: Chapter 11
I Samuel: Chapters 19-20
Psalm 126

H: _____
What gentle whisper did you hear as you read today?

E: _____
How did the passages encourage you?

A: _____
How can you apply what you learned in your day today?

R: _____
What do you need to receive from God? His love, mercy, grace, comfort, or something else?

Write your favorite verse from today's reading here:

_____

_____

DAILY PRAYER

Lord, help me hear Your gentle whispers as I read Your Word. Encourage me as I learn more about Your heart. Help me apply what I learn and act according to Your will. And help me receive all You have for me to receive from You today. In Jesus' name, Amen.

DAY 127:

Mark: Chapter 10
Hebrews: Chapter 12
I Samuel: Chapters 21-22
Psalm 127

H: _____
What gentle whisper did you hear as you read today?

E: _____
How did the passages encourage you?

A: _____
How can you apply what you learned in your day today?

R: _____
What do you need to receive from God? His love, mercy, grace, comfort, or something else?

Write your favorite verse from today's reading here:

_____
_____

DAY 128:

Mark: Chapter 11
Hebrews: Chapter 13
I Samuel: Chapters 23-24
Psalm 128

H: _____
What gentle whisper did you hear as you read today?

E: _____
How did the passages encourage you?

A: _____
How can you apply what you learned in your day today?

R: _____
What do you need to receive from God? His love, mercy, grace, comfort, or something else?

Write your favorite verse from today's reading here:

_____
_____

DAILY PRAYER

Lord, help me hear Your gentle whispers as I read Your Word. Encourage me as I learn more about Your heart. Help me apply what I learn and act according to Your will. And help me receive all You have for me to receive from You today. In Jesus' name, Amen.

DAY 129:

Mark: Chapter 12
James: Chapter 1
I Samuel: Chapters 25-26
Psalm 129

H: _____
What gentle whisper did you hear as you read today?

E: _____
How did the passages encourage you?

A: _____
How can you apply what you learned in your day today?

R: _____
What do you need to receive from God? His love, mercy, grace, comfort, or something else?

Write your favorite verse from today's reading here:

_____

_____

DAY 130:

Mark: Chapter 13
James: Chapter 2
I Samuel: Chapters 27-28
Psalm 130

H: _____
What gentle whisper did you hear as you read today?

E: _____
How did the passages encourage you?

A: _____
How can you apply what you learned in your day today?

R: _____
What do you need to receive from God? His love, mercy, grace, comfort, or something else?

Write your favorite verse from today's reading here:

_____

_____

DAILY PRAYER

Lord, help me hear Your gentle whispers as I read Your Word. Encourage me as I learn more about Your heart. Help me apply what I learn and act according to Your will. And help me receive all You have for me to receive from You today. In Jesus' name, Amen.

DAY 131:

Mark: Chapter 14
James: Chapter 3
I Samuel: Chapters 29-31
Psalm 131

H: _____
What gentle whisper did you hear as you read today?

E: _____
How did the passages encourage you?

A: _____
How can you apply what you learned in your day today?

R: _____
What do you need to receive from God? His love, mercy, grace, comfort, or something else?

Write your favorite verse from today's reading here:

_____

_____

DAY 132:

Mark: Chapter 15
James: Chapter 4
II Samuel: Chapters 1-2
Psalm 132

H: _____
What gentle whisper did you hear as you read today?

E: _____
How did the passages encourage you?

A: _____
How can you apply what you learned in your day today?

R: _____
What do you need to receive from God? His love, mercy, grace, comfort, or something else?

Write your favorite verse from today's reading here:

_____

_____

DAILY PRAYER

Lord, help me hear Your gentle whispers as I read Your Word. Encourage me as I learn more about Your heart. Help me apply what I learn and act according to Your will. And help me receive all You have for me to receive from You today. In Jesus' name, Amen.

DAY 133:

Mark: Chapter 16
James: Chapter 5
II Samuel: Chapters 3-4
Psalm 133

H: _____
What gentle whisper did you hear as you read today?

E: _____
How did the passages encourage you?

A: _____
How can you apply what you learned in your day today?

R: _____
What do you need to receive from God? His love, mercy, grace, comfort, or something else?

Write your favorite verse from today's reading here:

_____

_____

DAY 134:

Luke: Chapter 1
I Peter: Chapter 1
II Samuel: Chapters 5-6
Psalm 134

H: _____
What gentle whisper did you hear as you read today?

E: _____
How did the passages encourage you?

A: _____
How can you apply what you learned in your day today?

R: _____
What do you need to receive from God? His love, mercy, grace, comfort, or something else?

Write your favorite verse from today's reading here:

_____

_____

DAILY PRAYER

Lord, help me hear Your gentle whispers as I read Your Word. Encourage me as I learn more about Your heart. Help me apply what I learn and act according to Your will. And help me receive all You have for me to receive from You today. In Jesus' name, Amen.

DAY 135:

Luke: Chapter 2
I Peter: Chapter 2
II Samuel: Chapters 7-8
Psalm 135

H: _____
What gentle whisper did you hear as you read today?

E: _____
How did the passages encourage you?

A: _____
How can you apply what you learned in your day today?

R: _____
What do you need to receive from God? His love, mercy, grace, comfort, or something else?

Write your favorite verse from today's reading here:

_____

_____

DAY 136:

Luke: Chapter 3
I Peter: Chapter 3
II Samuel: Chapters 9-10
Psalm 136

H: _____
What gentle whisper did you hear as you read today?

E: _____
How did the passages encourage you?

A: _____
How can you apply what you learned in your day today?

R: _____
What do you need to receive from God? His love, mercy, grace, comfort, or something else?

Write your favorite verse from today's reading here:

_____

_____

DAILY PRAYER

Lord, help me hear Your gentle whispers as I read Your Word. Encourage me as I learn more about Your heart. Help me apply what I learn and act according to Your will. And help me receive all You have for me to receive from You today. In Jesus' name, Amen.

DAY 137:

Luke: Chapter 4
I Peter: Chapter 4
II Samuel: Chapters 11-12
Psalm 137

H: _____
What gentle whisper did you hear as you read today?

E: _____
How did the passages encourage you?

A: _____
How can you apply what you learned in your day today?

R: _____
What do you need to receive from God? His love, mercy, grace, comfort, or something else?

Write your favorite verse from today's reading here:

_____

_____

DAY 138:

Luke: Chapter 5
I Peter: Chapter 5
II Samuel: Chapters 13-14
Psalm 138

H: _____
What gentle whisper did you hear as you read today?

E: _____
How did the passages encourage you?

A: _____
How can you apply what you learned in your day today?

R: _____
What do you need to receive from God? His love, mercy, grace, comfort, or something else?

Write your favorite verse from today's reading here:

_____

_____

DAILY PRAYER

Lord, help me hear Your gentle whispers as I read Your Word. Encourage me as I learn more about Your heart. Help me apply what I learn and act according to Your will. And help me receive all You have for me to receive from You today. In Jesus' name, Amen.

DAY 139:

Luke: Chapter 6
II Peter: Chapter 1
II Samuel: Chapters 15-16
Psalm 139

H: _____
What gentle whisper did you hear as you read today?

E: _____
How did the passages encourage you?

A: _____
How can you apply what you learned in your day today?

R: _____
What do you need to receive from God? His love, mercy, grace, comfort, or something else?

Write your favorite verse from today's reading here:

_____
_____

DAY 140:

Luke: Chapter 7
II Peter: Chapter 2
II Samuel: Chapters 17-18
Psalm 140

H: _____
What gentle whisper did you hear as you read today?

E: _____
How did the passages encourage you?

A: _____
How can you apply what you learned in your day today?

R: _____
What do you need to receive from God? His love, mercy, grace, comfort, or something else?

Write your favorite verse from today's reading here:

_____
_____

DAILY PRAYER

Lord, help me hear Your gentle whispers as I read Your Word. Encourage me as I learn more about Your heart. Help me apply what I learn and act according to Your will. And help me receive all You have for me to receive from You today. In Jesus' name, Amen.

DAY 141:

Luke: Chapter 8
II Peter: Chapter 3
II Samuel: Chapters 19-20
Psalm 141

H: _____
What gentle whisper did you hear as you read today?

E: _____
How did the passages encourage you?

A: _____
How can you apply what you learned in your day today?

R: _____
What do you need to receive from God? His love, mercy, grace, comfort, or something else?

Write your favorite verse from today's reading here:

_____

_____

DAY 142:

Luke: Chapter 9
I John: Chapter 1
II Samuel: Chapters 21-22
Psalm 142

H: _____
What gentle whisper did you hear as you read today?

E: _____
How did the passages encourage you?

A: _____
How can you apply what you learned in your day today?

R: _____
What do you need to receive from God? His love, mercy, grace, comfort, or something else?

Write your favorite verse from today's reading here:

_____

_____

DAILY PRAYER

Lord, help me hear Your gentle whispers as I read Your Word. Encourage me as I learn more about Your heart. Help me apply what I learn and act according to Your will. And help me receive all You have for me to receive from You today. In Jesus' name, Amen.

DAY 143:

Luke: Chapter 10
I John: Chapter 2
II Samuel: Chapters 23-24
Psalm 143

H: _____
What gentle whisper did you hear as you read today?

E: _____
How did the passages encourage you?

A: _____
How can you apply what you learned in your day today?

R: _____
What do you need to receive from God? His love, mercy, grace, comfort, or something else?

Write your favorite verse from today's reading here:

_____
_____

DAY 144:

Luke: Chapter 11
I John: Chapter 3
I Kings: Chapters 1-2
Psalm 144

H: _____
What gentle whisper did you hear as you read today?

E: _____
How did the passages encourage you?

A: _____
How can you apply what you learned in your day today?

R: _____
What do you need to receive from God? His love, mercy, grace, comfort, or something else?

Write your favorite verse from today's reading here:

_____
_____

DAILY PRAYER

Lord, help me hear Your gentle whispers as I read Your Word. Encourage me as I learn more about Your heart. Help me apply what I learn and act according to Your will. And help me receive all You have for me to receive from You today. In Jesus' name, Amen.

DAY 145:

Luke: Chapter 12
I John: Chapter 4
I Kings: Chapters 3-4
Psalm 145

H: _____
What gentle whisper did you hear as you read today?

E: _____
How did the passages encourage you?

A: _____
How can you apply what you learned in your day today?

R: _____
What do you need to receive from God? His love, mercy, grace, comfort, or something else?

Write your favorite verse from today's reading here:

_____

_____

DAY 146:

Luke: Chapter 13
I John: Chapter 5
I Kings: Chapters 5-6
Psalm 146

H: _____
What gentle whisper did you hear as you read today?

E: _____
How did the passages encourage you?

A: _____
How can you apply what you learned in your day today?

R: _____
What do you need to receive from God? His love, mercy, grace, comfort, or something else?

Write your favorite verse from today's reading here:

_____

_____

DAILY PRAYER

Lord, help me hear Your gentle whispers as I read Your Word. Encourage me as I learn more about Your heart. Help me apply what I learn and act according to Your will. And help me receive all You have for me to receive from You today. In Jesus' name, Amen.

DAY 147:

Luke: Chapter 14
II John: Chapter 1
I Kings: Chapters 7-8
Psalm 147

H: _____
What gentle whisper did you hear as you read today?

E: _____
How did the passages encourage you?

A: _____
How can you apply what you learned in your day today?

R: _____
What do you need to receive from God? His love, mercy, grace, comfort, or something else?

Write your favorite verse from today's reading here:

_____

_____

DAY 148:

Luke: Chapter 15
III John: Chapter 1
I Kings: Chapters 9-10
Psalm 148

H: _____
What gentle whisper did you hear as you read today?

E: _____
How did the passages encourage you?

A: _____
How can you apply what you learned in your day today?

R: _____
What do you need to receive from God? His love, mercy, grace, comfort, or something else?

Write your favorite verse from today's reading here:

_____

_____

DAILY PRAYER

Lord, help me hear Your gentle whispers as I read Your Word. Encourage me as I learn more about Your heart. Help me apply what I learn and act according to Your will. And help me receive all You have for me to receive from You today. In Jesus' name, Amen.

DAY 149:

Luke: Chapter 16
Jude: Chapter 1
I Kings: Chapters 11-12
Psalm 149

H: _____
What gentle whisper did you hear as you read today?

E: _____
How did the passages encourage you?

A: _____
How can you apply what you learned in your day today?

R: _____
What do you need to receive from God? His love, mercy, grace, comfort, or something else?

Write your favorite verse from today's reading here:

_____
_____

DAY 150:

Luke: Chapter 17
Revelation: Chapter 1
I Kings: Chapters 13-14
Psalm 150

H: _____
What gentle whisper did you hear as you read today?

E: _____
How did the passages encourage you?

A: _____
How can you apply what you learned in your day today?

R: _____
What do you need to receive from God? His love, mercy, grace, comfort, or something else?

Write your favorite verse from today's reading here:

_____
_____

DAILY PRAYER

Lord, help me hear Your gentle whispers as I read Your Word. Encourage me as I learn more about Your heart. Help me apply what I learn and act according to Your will. And help me receive all You have for me to receive from You today. In Jesus' name, Amen.

DAY 151:

Luke: Chapter 18
Revelation: Chapter 2
I Kings: Chapters 15-16
Proverbs 1

H: _____
What gentle whisper did you hear as you read today?

E: _____
How did the passages encourage you?

A: _____
How can you apply what you learned in your day today?

R: _____
What do you need to receive from God? His love, mercy, grace, comfort, or something else?

Write your favorite verse from today's reading here:

_____
_____

DAY 152:

Luke: Chapter 19
Revelation: Chapter 3
I Kings: Chapters 17-18
Proverbs 2

H: _____
What gentle whisper did you hear as you read today?

E: _____
How did the passages encourage you?

A: _____
How can you apply what you learned in your day today?

R: _____
What do you need to receive from God? His love, mercy, grace, comfort, or something else?

Write your favorite verse from today's reading here:

_____
_____

DAILY PRAYER

Lord, help me hear Your gentle whispers as I read Your Word. Encourage me as I learn more about Your heart. Help me apply what I learn and act according to Your will. And help me receive all You have for me to receive from You today. In Jesus' name, Amen.

DAY 153:

Luke: Chapter 20
Revelation: Chapter 4
I Kings: Chapters 19-20
Proverbs 3

H: _____
What gentle whisper did you hear as you read today?

E: _____
How did the passages encourage you?

A: _____
How can you apply what you learned in your day today?

R: _____
What do you need to receive from God? His love, mercy, grace, comfort, or something else?

Write your favorite verse from today's reading here:

_____

DAY 154:

Luke: Chapter 21
Revelation: Chapter 5
I Kings: Chapters 21-22
Proverbs 4

H: _____
What gentle whisper did you hear as you read today?

E: _____
How did the passages encourage you?

A: _____
How can you apply what you learned in your day today?

R: _____
What do you need to receive from God? His love, mercy, grace, comfort, or something else?

Write your favorite verse from today's reading here:

_____

DAILY PRAYER

Lord, help me hear Your gentle whispers as I read Your Word. Encourage me as I learn more about Your heart. Help me apply what I learn and act according to Your will. And help me receive all You have for me to receive from You today. In Jesus' name, Amen.

DAY 155:

Luke: Chapter 22
Revelation: Chapter 6
II Kings: Chapters 1-2
Proverbs 5

H: _____
What gentle whisper did you hear as you read today?

E: _____
How did the passages encourage you?

A: _____
How can you apply what you learned in your day today?

R: _____
What do you need to receive from God? His love, mercy, grace, comfort, or something else?

Write your favorite verse from today's reading here:

_____

_____

DAY 156:

Luke: Chapter 23
Revelation: Chapter 7
II Kings: Chapters 3-4
Proverbs 6

H: _____
What gentle whisper did you hear as you read today?

E: _____
How did the passages encourage you?

A: _____
How can you apply what you learned in your day today?

R: _____
What do you need to receive from God? His love, mercy, grace, comfort, or something else?

Write your favorite verse from today's reading here:

_____

_____

DAILY PRAYER

Lord, help me hear Your gentle whispers as I read Your Word. Encourage me as I learn more about Your heart. Help me apply what I learn and act according to Your will. And help me receive all You have for me to receive from You today. In Jesus' name, Amen.

DAY 157:

Luke: Chapter 24
Revelation: Chapter 8
II Kings: Chapters 5-6
Proverbs 7

H: _____
What gentle whisper did you hear as you read today?

E: _____
How did the passages encourage you?

A: _____
How can you apply what you learned in your day today?

R: _____
What do you need to receive from God? His love, mercy, grace, comfort, or something else?

Write your favorite verse from today's reading here:

_____

_____

DAY 158:

John: Chapter 1
Revelation: Chapter 9
II Kings: Chapters 7-8
Proverbs 8

H: _____
What gentle whisper did you hear as you read today?

E: _____
How did the passages encourage you?

A: _____
How can you apply what you learned in your day today?

R: _____
What do you need to receive from God? His love, mercy, grace, comfort, or something else?

Write your favorite verse from today's reading here:

_____

_____

DAILY PRAYER

Lord, help me hear Your gentle whispers as I read Your Word. Encourage me as I learn more about Your heart. Help me apply what I learn and act according to Your will. And help me receive all You have for me to receive from You today. In Jesus' name, Amen.

DAY 159:

John: Chapter 2
Revelation: Chapter 10
II Kings: Chapters 9-10
Proverbs 9

H: _____
What gentle whisper did you hear as you read today?

E: _____
How did the passages encourage you?

A: _____
How can you apply what you learned in your day today?

R: _____
What do you need to receive from God? His love, mercy, grace, comfort, or something else?

Write your favorite verse from today's reading here:

_____

_____

DAY 160:

John: Chapter 3
Revelation: Chapter 11
II Kings: Chapters 11-12
Proverbs 10

H: _____
What gentle whisper did you hear as you read today?

E: _____
How did the passages encourage you?

A: _____
How can you apply what you learned in your day today?

R: _____
What do you need to receive from God? His love, mercy, grace, comfort, or something else?

Write your favorite verse from today's reading here:

_____

_____

DAILY PRAYER

Lord, help me hear Your gentle whispers as I read Your Word. Encourage me as I learn more about Your heart. Help me apply what I learn and act according to Your will. And help me receive all You have for me to receive from You today. In Jesus' name, Amen.

DAY 161:

John: Chapter 4
Revelation: Chapter 12
II Kings: Chapters 13-14
Proverbs 11

H: _____
What gentle whisper did you hear as you read today?

E: _____
How did the passages encourage you?

A: _____
How can you apply what you learned in your day today?

R: _____
What do you need to receive from God? His love, mercy, grace, comfort, or something else?

Write your favorite verse from today's reading here:

_____

_____

DAY 162:

John: Chapter 5
Revelation: Chapter 13
II Kings: Chapters 15-16
Proverbs 12

H: _____
What gentle whisper did you hear as you read today?

E: _____
How did the passages encourage you?

A: _____
How can you apply what you learned in your day today?

R: _____
What do you need to receive from God? His love, mercy, grace, comfort, or something else?

Write your favorite verse from today's reading here:

_____

_____

DAILY PRAYER

Lord, help me hear Your gentle whispers as I read Your Word. Encourage me as I learn more about Your heart. Help me apply what I learn and act according to Your will. And help me receive all You have for me to receive from You today. In Jesus' name, Amen.

DAY 163:

John: Chapter 6
Revelation: Chapter 14
II Kings: Chapters 17-18
Proverbs 13

H: _____
What gentle whisper did you hear as you read today?

E: _____
How did the passages encourage you?

A: _____
How can you apply what you learned in your day today?

R: _____
What do you need to receive from God? His love, mercy, grace, comfort, or something else?

Write your favorite verse from today's reading here:

_____

_____

DAY 164:

John: Chapter 7
Revelation: Chapter 15
II Kings: Chapters 19-20
Proverbs 14

H: _____
What gentle whisper did you hear as you read today?

E: _____
How did the passages encourage you?

A: _____
How can you apply what you learned in your day today?

R: _____
What do you need to receive from God? His love, mercy, grace, comfort, or something else?

Write your favorite verse from today's reading here:

_____

_____

DAILY PRAYER

Lord, help me hear Your gentle whispers as I read Your Word. Encourage me as I learn more about Your heart. Help me apply what I learn and act according to Your will. And help me receive all You have for me to receive from You today. In Jesus' name, Amen.

DAY 165:

John: Chapter 8
Revelation: Chapter 16
II Kings: Chapters 21-22
Proverbs 15

H: _____
What gentle whisper did you hear as you read today?

E: _____
How did the passages encourage you?

A: _____
How can you apply what you learned in your day today?

R: _____
What do you need to receive from God? His love, mercy, grace, comfort, or something else?

Write your favorite verse from today's reading here:

_____

_____

DAY 166:

John: Chapter 9
Revelation: Chapter 17
II Kings: Chapters 23-25
Proverbs 16

H: _____
What gentle whisper did you hear as you read today?

E: _____
How did the passages encourage you?

A: _____
How can you apply what you learned in your day today?

R: _____
What do you need to receive from God? His love, mercy, grace, comfort, or something else?

Write your favorite verse from today's reading here:

_____

_____

DAILY PRAYER

Lord, help me hear Your gentle whispers as I read Your Word. Encourage me as I learn more about Your heart. Help me apply what I learn and act according to Your will. And help me receive all You have for me to receive from You today. In Jesus' name, Amen.

DAY 167:

John: Chapter 10
Revelation: Chapter 18
I Chronicles: Chapters 1-2
Proverbs 17

H: _____
What gentle whisper did you hear as you read today?

E: _____
How did the passages encourage you?

A: _____
How can you apply what you learned in your day today?

R: _____
What do you need to receive from God? His love, mercy, grace, comfort, or something else?

Write your favorite verse from today's reading here:

_____
_____

DAY 168:

John: Chapter 11
Revelation: Chapter 19
I Chronicles: Chapters 3-4
Proverbs 18

H: _____
What gentle whisper did you hear as you read today?

E: _____
How did the passages encourage you?

A: _____
How can you apply what you learned in your day today?

R: _____
What do you need to receive from God? His love, mercy, grace, comfort, or something else?

Write your favorite verse from today's reading here:

_____
_____

DAILY PRAYER

Lord, help me hear Your gentle whispers as I read Your Word. Encourage me as I learn more about Your heart. Help me apply what I learn and act according to Your will. And help me receive all You have for me to receive from You today. In Jesus' name, Amen.

DAY 169:

John: Chapter 12
Revelation: Chapter 20
I Chronicles: Chapters 5-6
Proverbs 19

H: _____
What gentle whisper did you hear as you read today?

E: _____
How did the passages encourage you?

A: _____
How can you apply what you learned in your day today?

R: _____
What do you need to receive from God? His love, mercy, grace, comfort, or something else?

Write your favorite verse from today's reading here:

_____

_____

DAY 170:

John: Chapter 13
Revelation: Chapter 21
I Chronicles: Chapters 7-8
Proverbs 20

H: _____
What gentle whisper did you hear as you read today?

E: _____
How did the passages encourage you?

A: _____
How can you apply what you learned in your day today?

R: _____
What do you need to receive from God? His love, mercy, grace, comfort, or something else?

Write your favorite verse from today's reading here:

_____

_____

DAILY PRAYER

Lord, help me hear Your gentle whispers as I read Your Word. Encourage me as I learn more about Your heart. Help me apply what I learn and act according to Your will. And help me receive all You have for me to receive from You today. In Jesus' name, Amen.

DAY 171:

John: Chapter 14
Revelation: Chapter 22
I Chronicles: Chapters 9-10
Proverbs 21

H: _____
What gentle whisper did you hear as you read today?

E: _____
How did the passages encourage you?

A: _____
How can you apply what you learned in your day today?

R: _____
What do you need to receive from God? His love, mercy, grace, comfort, or something else?

Write your favorite verse from today's reading here:

_____

_____

DAY 172:

John: Chapter 15
Acts: Chapter 1
I Chronicles: Chapters 11-12
Proverbs 22

H: _____
What gentle whisper did you hear as you read today?

E: _____
How did the passages encourage you?

A: _____
How can you apply what you learned in your day today?

R: _____
What do you need to receive from God? His love, mercy, grace, comfort, or something else?

Write your favorite verse from today's reading here:

_____

_____

DAILY PRAYER

Lord, help me hear Your gentle whispers as I read Your Word. Encourage me as I learn more about Your heart. Help me apply what I learn and act according to Your will. And help me receive all You have for me to receive from You today. In Jesus' name, Amen.

DAY 173:

John: Chapter 16
Acts: Chapter 2
I Chronicles: Chapters 13-14
Proverbs 23

H: _____
What gentle whisper did you hear as you read today?

E: _____
How did the passages encourage you?

A: _____
How can you apply what you learned in your day today?

R: _____
What do you need to receive from God? His love, mercy, grace, comfort, or something else?

Write your favorite verse from today's reading here:

_____

_____

DAY 174:

John: Chapter 17
Acts: Chapter 3
I Chronicles: Chapters 15-16
Proverbs 24

H: _____
What gentle whisper did you hear as you read today?

E: _____
How did the passages encourage you?

A: _____
How can you apply what you learned in your day today?

R: _____
What do you need to receive from God? His love, mercy, grace, comfort, or something else?

Write your favorite verse from today's reading here:

_____

_____

DAILY PRAYER

Lord, help me hear Your gentle whispers as I read Your Word. Encourage me as I learn more about Your heart. Help me apply what I learn and act according to Your will. And help me receive all You have for me to receive from You today. In Jesus' name, Amen.

DAY 175:

John: Chapter 18
Acts: Chapter 4
I Chronicles: Chapters 17-18
Proverbs 25

H: _____
What gentle whisper did you hear as you read today?

E: _____
How did the passages encourage you?

A: _____
How can you apply what you learned in your day today?

R: _____
What do you need to receive from God? His love, mercy, grace, comfort, or something else?

Write your favorite verse from today's reading here:

_____
_____

DAY 176:

John: Chapter 19
Acts: Chapter 5
I Chronicles: Chapters 19-20
Proverbs 26

H: _____
What gentle whisper did you hear as you read today?

E: _____
How did the passages encourage you?

A: _____
How can you apply what you learned in your day today?

R: _____
What do you need to receive from God? His love, mercy, grace, comfort, or something else?

Write your favorite verse from today's reading here:

_____
_____

DAILY PRAYER

Lord, help me hear Your gentle whispers as I read Your Word. Encourage me as I learn more about Your heart. Help me apply what I learn and act according to Your will. And help me receive all You have for me to receive from You today. In Jesus' name, Amen.

DAY 177:

John: Chapter 20
Acts: Chapter 6
I Chronicles: Chapters
21-22
Proverbs 27

H: _____
What gentle whisper did you hear as you read today?

E: _____
How did the passages encourage you?

A: _____
How can you apply what you learned in your day today?

R: _____
What do you need to receive from God? His love, mercy, grace, comfort, or something else?

Write your favorite verse from today's reading here:

_____

_____

DAY 178:

John: Chapter 21
Acts: Chapter 7
I Chronicles: Chapters
23-24
Proverbs 28

H: _____
What gentle whisper did you hear as you read today?

E: _____
How did the passages encourage you?

A: _____
How can you apply what you learned in your day today?

R: _____
What do you need to receive from God? His love, mercy, grace, comfort, or something else?

Write your favorite verse from today's reading here:

_____

_____

DAILY PRAYER

Lord, help me hear Your gentle whispers as I read Your Word. Encourage me as I learn more about Your heart. Help me apply what I learn and act according to Your will. And help me receive all You have for me to receive from You today. In Jesus' name, Amen.

DAY 179:

Matthew: Chapter 1
Acts: Chapter 8
I Chronicles: Chapters 25-26
Proverbs 29

H: _____
What gentle whisper did you hear as you read today?

E: _____
How did the passages encourage you?

A: _____
How can you apply what you learned in your day today?

R: _____
What do you need to receive from God? His love, mercy, grace, comfort, or something else?

Write your favorite verse from today's reading here:

_____

_____

DAY 180:

Matthew: Chapter 2
Acts: Chapter 9
I Chronicles: Chapters 27-29
Proverbs 30

H: _____
What gentle whisper did you hear as you read today?

E: _____
How did the passages encourage you?

A: _____
How can you apply what you learned in your day today?

R: _____
What do you need to receive from God? His love, mercy, grace, comfort, or something else?

Write your favorite verse from today's reading here:

_____

_____

DAILY PRAYER

Lord, help me hear Your gentle whispers as I read Your Word. Encourage me as I learn more about Your heart. Help me apply what I learn and act according to Your will. And help me receive all You have for me to receive from You today. In Jesus' name, Amen.

DAY 181:

Matthew: Chapter 3
Acts: Chapter 10
II Chronicles: Chapters 1-2
Proverbs 31

H: _____
What gentle whisper did you hear as you read today?

E: _____
How did the passages encourage you?

A: _____
How can you apply what you learned in your day today?

R: _____
What do you need to receive from God? His love, mercy, grace, comfort, or something else?

Write your favorite verse from today's reading here:

_____

_____

DAY 182:

Matthew: Chapter 4
Acts: Chapter 11
II Chronicles: Chapters 3-4
Psalm 1

H: _____
What gentle whisper did you hear as you read today?

E: _____
How did the passages encourage you?

A: _____
How can you apply what you learned in your day today?

R: _____
What do you need to receive from God? His love, mercy, grace, comfort, or something else?

Write your favorite verse from today's reading here:

_____

_____

DAILY PRAYER

Lord, help me hear Your gentle whispers as I read Your Word. Encourage me as I learn more about Your heart. Help me apply what I learn and act according to Your will. And help me receive all You have for me to receive from You today. In Jesus' name, Amen.

DAY 183:

Matthew: Chapter 5
Acts: Chapter 12
II Chronicles: Chapters 5-6
Psalm 2

H: _____
What gentle whisper did you hear as you read today?

E: _____
How did the passages encourage you?

A: _____
How can you apply what you learned in your day today?

R: _____
What do you need to receive from God? His love, mercy, grace, comfort, or something else?

Write your favorite verse from today's reading here:

_____
_____

DAY 184:

Matthew: Chapter 6
Acts: Chapter 13
II Chronicles: Chapters 7-8
Psalm 3

H: _____
What gentle whisper did you hear as you read today?

E: _____
How did the passages encourage you?

A: _____
How can you apply what you learned in your day today?

R: _____
What do you need to receive from God? His love, mercy, grace, comfort, or something else?

Write your favorite verse from today's reading here:

_____
_____

DAILY PRAYER

Lord, help me hear Your gentle whispers as I read Your Word. Encourage me as I learn more about Your heart. Help me apply what I learn and act according to Your will. And help me receive all You have for me to receive from You today. In Jesus' name, Amen.

DAY 185:

Matthew: Chapter 7
Acts: Chapter 14
II Chronicles: Chapters 9-10
Psalm 4

H: _____
What gentle whisper did you hear as you read today?

E: _____
How did the passages encourage you?

A: _____
How can you apply what you learned in your day today?

R: _____
What do you need to receive from God? His love, mercy, grace, comfort, or something else?

Write your favorite verse from today's reading here:

_____

_____

DAY 186:

Matthew: Chapter 8
Acts: Chapter 15
II Chronicles: Chapters 11-12
Psalm 5

H: _____
What gentle whisper did you hear as you read today?

E: _____
How did the passages encourage you?

A: _____
How can you apply what you learned in your day today?

R: _____
What do you need to receive from God? His love, mercy, grace, comfort, or something else?

Write your favorite verse from today's reading here:

_____

_____

DAILY PRAYER

Lord, help me hear Your gentle whispers as I read Your Word. Encourage me as I learn more about Your heart. Help me apply what I learn and act according to Your will. And help me receive all You have for me to receive from You today. In Jesus' name, Amen.

DAY 187:

Matthew: Chapter 9
Acts: Chapter 16
II Chronicles: Chapters 13-14
Psalm 6

H: _____
What gentle whisper did you hear as you read today?

E: _____
How did the passages encourage you?

A: _____
How can you apply what you learned in your day today?

R: _____
What do you need to receive from God? His love, mercy, grace, comfort, or something else?

Write your favorite verse from today's reading here:

_____
_____

DAY 188:

Matthew: Chapter 10
Acts: Chapter 17
II Chronicles: Chapters 15-16
Psalm 7

H: _____
What gentle whisper did you hear as you read today?

E: _____
How did the passages encourage you?

A: _____
How can you apply what you learned in your day today?

R: _____
What do you need to receive from God? His love, mercy, grace, comfort, or something else?

Write your favorite verse from today's reading here:

_____
_____

DAILY PRAYER

Lord, help me hear Your gentle whispers as I read Your Word. Encourage me as I learn more about Your heart. Help me apply what I learn and act according to Your will. And help me receive all You have for me to receive from You today. In Jesus' name, Amen.

DAY 189:

Matthew: Chapter 11
Acts: Chapter 18
II Chronicles: Chapters 17-18
Psalm 8

H: _____
What gentle whisper did you hear as you read today?

E: _____
How did the passages encourage you?

A: _____
How can you apply what you learned in your day today?

R: _____
What do you need to receive from God? His love, mercy, grace, comfort, or something else?

Write your favorite verse from today's reading here:

_____

_____

DAY 190:

Matthew: Chapter 12
Acts: Chapter 19
II Chronicles: Chapters 19-20
Psalm 9

H: _____
What gentle whisper did you hear as you read today?

E: _____
How did the passages encourage you?

A: _____
How can you apply what you learned in your day today?

R: _____
What do you need to receive from God? His love, mercy, grace, comfort, or something else?

Write your favorite verse from today's reading here:

_____

_____

DAILY PRAYER

Lord, help me hear Your gentle whispers as I read Your Word. Encourage me as I learn more about Your heart. Help me apply what I learn and act according to Your will. And help me receive all You have for me to receive from You today. In Jesus' name, Amen.

DAY 191:

Matthew: Chapter 13
Acts: Chapter 20
II Chronicles: Chapters 21-22
Psalm 10

H: _____
What gentle whisper did you hear as you read today?

E: _____
How did the passages encourage you?

A: _____
How can you apply what you learned in your day today?

R: _____
What do you need to receive from God? His love, mercy, grace, comfort, or something else?

Write your favorite verse from today's reading here:

_____
_____

DAY 192:

Matthew: Chapter 14
Acts: Chapter 21
II Chronicles: Chapters 23-24
Psalm 11

H: _____
What gentle whisper did you hear as you read today?

E: _____
How did the passages encourage you?

A: _____
How can you apply what you learned in your day today?

R: _____
What do you need to receive from God? His love, mercy, grace, comfort, or something else?

Write your favorite verse from today's reading here:

_____
_____

DAILY PRAYER

Lord, help me hear Your gentle whispers as I read Your Word. Encourage me as I learn more about Your heart. Help me apply what I learn and act according to Your will. And help me receive all You have for me to receive from You today. In Jesus' name, Amen.

DAY 193:

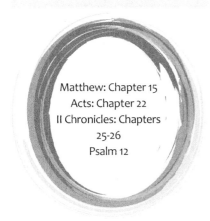

Matthew: Chapter 15
Acts: Chapter 22
II Chronicles: Chapters 25-26
Psalm 12

H: _____
What gentle whisper did you hear as you read today?

E: _____
How did the passages encourage you?

A: _____
How can you apply what you learned in your day today?

R: _____
What do you need to receive from God? His love, mercy, grace, comfort, or something else?

Write your favorite verse from today's reading here:

_____

_____

DAY 194:

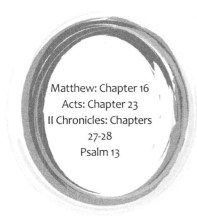

Matthew: Chapter 16
Acts: Chapter 23
II Chronicles: Chapters 27-28
Psalm 13

H: _____
What gentle whisper did you hear as you read today?

E: _____
How did the passages encourage you?

A: _____
How can you apply what you learned in your day today?

R: _____
What do you need to receive from God? His love, mercy, grace, comfort, or something else?

Write your favorite verse from today's reading here:

_____

_____

DAILY PRAYER

Lord, help me hear Your gentle whispers as I read Your Word. Encourage me as I learn more about Your heart. Help me apply what I learn and act according to Your will. And help me receive all You have for me to receive from You today. In Jesus' name, Amen.

DAY 195:

Matthew: Chapter 17
Acts: Chapter 24
II Chronicles: Chapters 29-30
Psalm 14

H: _____
What gentle whisper did you hear as you read today?

E: _____
How did the passages encourage you?

A: _____
How can you apply what you learned in your day today?

R: _____
What do you need to receive from God? His love, mercy, grace, comfort, or something else?

Write your favorite verse from today's reading here:

_____
_____

DAY 196:

Matthew: Chapter 18
Acts: Chapter 25
II Chronicles: Chapters 31-32
Psalm 15

H: _____
What gentle whisper did you hear as you read today?

E: _____
How did the passages encourage you?

A: _____
How can you apply what you learned in your day today?

R: _____
What do you need to receive from God? His love, mercy, grace, comfort, or something else?

Write your favorite verse from today's reading here:

_____
_____

DAILY PRAYER

Lord, help me hear Your gentle whispers as I read Your Word. Encourage me as I learn more about Your heart. Help me apply what I learn and act according to Your will. And help me receive all You have for me to receive from You today. In Jesus' name, Amen.

DAY 197:

Matthew: Chapter 19
Acts: Chapter 26
II Chronicles: Chapters 33-34
Psalm 16

H: _____
What gentle whisper did you hear as you read today?

E: _____
How did the passages encourage you?

A: _____
How can you apply what you learned in your day today?

R: _____
What do you need to receive from God? His love, mercy, grace, comfort, or something else?

Write your favorite verse from today's reading here:

_____
_____

DAY 198:

Matthew: Chapter 20
Acts: Chapter 27
II Chronicles: Chapters 35-36
Psalm 17

H: _____
What gentle whisper did you hear as you read today?

E: _____
How did the passages encourage you?

A: _____
How can you apply what you learned in your day today?

R: _____
What do you need to receive from God? His love, mercy, grace, comfort, or something else?

Write your favorite verse from today's reading here:

_____
_____

DAILY PRAYER

Lord, help me hear Your gentle whispers as I read Your Word. Encourage me as I learn more about Your heart. Help me apply what I learn and act according to Your will. And help me receive all You have for me to receive from You today. In Jesus' name, Amen.

DAY 199:

Matthew: Chapter 21
Acts: Chapter 28
Ezra: Chapters 1-2
Psalm 18

H: _____
What gentle whisper did you hear as you read today?

E: _____
How did the passages encourage you?

A: _____
How can you apply what you learned in your day today?

R: _____
What do you need to receive from God? His love, mercy, grace, comfort, or something else?

Write your favorite verse from today's reading here:

_____
_____

DAY 200:

Matthew: Chapter 22
Romans: Chapter 1
Ezra: Chapters 3-4
Psalm 19

H: _____
What gentle whisper did you hear as you read today?

E: _____
How did the passages encourage you?

A: _____
How can you apply what you learned in your day today?

R: _____
What do you need to receive from God? His love, mercy, grace, comfort, or something else?

Write your favorite verse from today's reading here:

_____
_____

DAILY PRAYER

Lord, help me hear Your gentle whispers as I read Your Word. Encourage me as I learn more about Your heart. Help me apply what I learn and act according to Your will. And help me receive all You have for me to receive from You today. In Jesus' name, Amen.

DAY 201:

Matthew: Chapter 23
Romans: Chapter 2
Ezra: Chapters 5-6
Psalm 20

H: _____
What gentle whisper did you hear as you read today?

E: _____
How did the passages encourage you?

A: _____
How can you apply what you learned in your day today?

R: _____
What do you need to receive from God? His love, mercy, grace, comfort, or something else?

Write your favorite verse from today's reading here:

_____

_____

DAY 202:

Matthew: Chapter 24
Romans: Chapter 3
Ezra: Chapters 7-8
Psalm 21

H: _____
What gentle whisper did you hear as you read today?

E: _____
How did the passages encourage you?

A: _____
How can you apply what you learned in your day today?

R: _____
What do you need to receive from God? His love, mercy, grace, comfort, or something else?

Write your favorite verse from today's reading here:

_____

_____

DAILY PRAYER

Lord, help me hear Your gentle whispers as I read Your Word. Encourage me as I learn more about Your heart. Help me apply what I learn and act according to Your will. And help me receive all You have for me to receive from You today. In Jesus' name, Amen.

DAY 203:

Matthew: Chapter 25
Romans: Chapter 4
Ezra: Chapters 9-10
Psalm 22

H: _____
What gentle whisper did you hear as you read today?

E: _____
How did the passages encourage you?

A: _____
How can you apply what you learned in your day today?

R: _____
What do you need to receive from God? His love, mercy, grace, comfort, or something else?

Write your favorite verse from today's reading here:

_____

_____

DAY 204:

Matthew: Chapter 26
Romans: Chapter 5
Nehemiah: Chapters 1-2
Psalm 23

H: _____
What gentle whisper did you hear as you read today?

E: _____
How did the passages encourage you?

A: _____
How can you apply what you learned in your day today?

R: _____
What do you need to receive from God? His love, mercy, grace, comfort, or something else?

Write your favorite verse from today's reading here:

_____

_____

DAILY PRAYER

Lord, help me hear Your gentle whispers as I read Your Word. Encourage me as I learn more about Your heart. Help me apply what I learn and act according to Your will. And help me receive all You have for me to receive from You today. In Jesus' name, Amen.

DAY 205:

Matthew: Chapter 27
Romans: Chapter 6
Nehemiah: Chapters 3-4
Psalm 24

H: _____
What gentle whisper did you hear as you read today?

E: _____
How did the passages encourage you?

A: _____
How can you apply what you learned in your day today?

R: _____
What do you need to receive from God? His love, mercy, grace, comfort, or something else?

Write your favorite verse from today's reading here:

_____

_____

DAY 206:

Matthew: Chapter 28
Romans: Chapter 7
Nehemiah: Chapters 5-6
Psalm 25

H: _____
What gentle whisper did you hear as you read today?

E: _____
How did the passages encourage you?

A: _____
How can you apply what you learned in your day today?

R: _____
What do you need to receive from God? His love, mercy, grace, comfort, or something else?

Write your favorite verse from today's reading here:

_____

_____

DAILY PRAYER

Lord, help me hear Your gentle whispers as I read Your Word. Encourage me as I learn more about Your heart. Help me apply what I learn and act according to Your will. And help me receive all You have for me to receive from You today. In Jesus' name, Amen.

DAY 207:

Mark: Chapter 1
Romans: Chapter 8
Nehemiah: Chapters 7-8
Psalm 26

H: _____
What gentle whisper did you hear as you read today?

E: _____
How did the passages encourage you?

A: _____
How can you apply what you learned in your day today?

R: _____
What do you need to receive from God? His love, mercy, grace, comfort, or something else?

Write your favorite verse from today's reading here:

_____
_____

DAY 208:

Mark: Chapter 2
Romans: Chapter 9
Nehemiah: Chapters 9-10
Psalm 27

H: _____
What gentle whisper did you hear as you read today?

E: _____
How did the passages encourage you?

A: _____
How can you apply what you learned in your day today?

R: _____
What do you need to receive from God? His love, mercy, grace, comfort, or something else?

Write your favorite verse from today's reading here:

_____
_____

DAILY PRAYER

Lord, help me hear Your gentle whispers as I read Your Word. Encourage me as I learn more about Your heart. Help me apply what I learn and act according to Your will. And help me receive all You have for me to receive from You today. In Jesus' name, Amen.

DAY 209:

Mark: Chapter 3
Romans: Chapter 10
Nehemiah: Chapters 11-13
Psalm 28

H: _____
What gentle whisper did you hear as you read today?

E: _____
How did the passages encourage you?

A: _____
How can you apply what you learned in your day today?

R: _____
What do you need to receive from God? His love, mercy, grace, comfort, or something else?

Write your favorite verse from today's reading here:

_____
_____

DAY 210:

Mark: Chapter 4
Romans: Chapter 11
Esther: Chapters 1-2
Psalm 29

H: _____
What gentle whisper did you hear as you read today?

E: _____
How did the passages encourage you?

A: _____
How can you apply what you learned in your day today?

R: _____
What do you need to receive from God? His love, mercy, grace, comfort, or something else?

Write your favorite verse from today's reading here:

_____
_____

DAILY PRAYER

Lord, help me hear Your gentle whispers as I read Your Word. Encourage me as I learn more about Your heart. Help me apply what I learn and act according to Your will. And help me receive all You have for me to receive from You today. In Jesus' name, Amen.

DAY 211:

Mark: Chapter 5
Romans: Chapter 12
Esther: Chapters 3-4
Psalm 30

H: _____
What gentle whisper did you hear as you read today?

E: _____
How did the passages encourage you?

A: _____
How can you apply what you learned in your day today?

R: _____
What do you need to receive from God? His love, mercy, grace, comfort, or something else?

Write your favorite verse from today's reading here:

_____

_____

DAY 212:

Mark: Chapter 6
Romans: Chapter 13
Esther: Chapters 5-6
Psalm 31

H: _____
What gentle whisper did you hear as you read today?

E: _____
How did the passages encourage you?

A: _____
How can you apply what you learned in your day today?

R: _____
What do you need to receive from God? His love, mercy, grace, comfort, or something else?

Write your favorite verse from today's reading here:

_____

_____

DAILY PRAYER

Lord, help me hear Your gentle whispers as I read Your Word. Encourage me as I learn more about Your heart. Help me apply what I learn and act according to Your will. And help me receive all You have for me to receive from You today. In Jesus' name, Amen.

DAY 213:

Mark: Chapter 7
Romans: Chapter 14
Esther: Chapters 7-8
Psalm 32

H: _____
What gentle whisper did you hear as you read today?

E: _____
How did the passages encourage you?

A: _____
How can you apply what you learned in your day today?

R: _____
What do you need to receive from God? His love, mercy, grace, comfort, or something else?

Write your favorite verse from today's reading here:

_____
_____

DAY 214:

Mark: Chapter 8
Romans: Chapter 15
Esther: Chapters 9-10
Psalm 33

H: _____
What gentle whisper did you hear as you read today?

E: _____
How did the passages encourage you?

A: _____
How can you apply what you learned in your day today?

R: _____
What do you need to receive from God? His love, mercy, grace, comfort, or something else?

Write your favorite verse from today's reading here:

_____
_____

DAILY PRAYER

Lord, help me hear Your gentle whispers as I read Your Word. Encourage me as I learn more about Your heart. Help me apply what I learn and act according to Your will. And help me receive all You have for me to receive from You today. In Jesus' name, Amen.

DAY 215:

Mark: Chapter 9
Romans: Chapter 16
Job: Chapters 1-2
Psalm 34

H: _____
What gentle whisper did you hear as you read today?

E: _____
How did the passages encourage you?

A: _____
How can you apply what you learned in your day today?

R: _____
What do you need to receive from God? His love, mercy, grace, comfort, or something else?

Write your favorite verse from today's reading here:

_____
_____

DAY 216:

Mark: Chapter 10
I Corinthians: Chapter 1
Job: Chapters 3-4
Psalm 35

H: _____
What gentle whisper did you hear as you read today?

E: _____
How did the passages encourage you?

A: _____
How can you apply what you learned in your day today?

R: _____
What do you need to receive from God? His love, mercy, grace, comfort, or something else?

Write your favorite verse from today's reading here:

_____
_____

DAILY PRAYER

Lord, help me hear Your gentle whispers as I read Your Word. Encourage me as I learn more about Your heart. Help me apply what I learn and act according to Your will. And help me receive all You have for me to receive from You today. In Jesus' name, Amen.

DAY 217:

Mark: Chapter 11
I Corinthians: Chapter 2
Job: Chapters 5-6
Psalm 36

H: _____
What gentle whisper did you hear as you read today?

E: _____
How did the passages encourage you?

A: _____
How can you apply what you learned in your day today?

R: _____
What do you need to receive from God? His love, mercy, grace, comfort, or something else?

Write your favorite verse from today's reading here:

_____

_____

DAY 218:

Mark: Chapter 12
I Corinthians: Chapter 3
Job: Chapters 7-8
Psalm 37

H: _____
What gentle whisper did you hear as you read today?

E: _____
How did the passages encourage you?

A: _____
How can you apply what you learned in your day today?

R: _____
What do you need to receive from God? His love, mercy, grace, comfort, or something else?

Write your favorite verse from today's reading here:

_____

_____

DAILY PRAYER

Lord, help me hear Your gentle whispers as I read Your Word. Encourage me as I learn more about Your heart. Help me apply what I learn and act according to Your will. And help me receive all You have for me to receive from You today. In Jesus' name, Amen.

DAY 219:

Mark: Chapter 13
I Corinthians: Chapter 4
Job: Chapters 9-10
Psalm 38

H: _____
What gentle whisper did you hear as you read today?

E: _____
How did the passages encourage you?

A: _____
How can you apply what you learned in your day today?

R: _____
What do you need to receive from God? His love, mercy, grace, comfort, or something else?

Write your favorite verse from today's reading here:

_____

_____

DAY 220:

Mark: Chapter 14
I Corinthians: Chapter 5
Job: Chapters 11-12
Psalm 39

H: _____
What gentle whisper did you hear as you read today?

E: _____
How did the passages encourage you?

A: _____
How can you apply what you learned in your day today?

R: _____
What do you need to receive from God? His love, mercy, grace, comfort, or something else?

Write your favorite verse from today's reading here:

_____

_____

DAILY PRAYER

Lord, help me hear Your gentle whispers as I read Your Word. Encourage me as I learn more about Your heart. Help me apply what I learn and act according to Your will. And help me receive all You have for me to receive from You today. In Jesus' name, Amen.

DAY 221:

Mark: Chapter 15
I Corinthians: Chapter 6
Job: Chapters 13-14
Psalm 40

H: _____
What gentle whisper did you hear as you read today?

E: _____
How did the passages encourage you?

A: _____
How can you apply what you learned in your day today?

R: _____
What do you need to receive from God? His love, mercy, grace, comfort, or something else?

Write your favorite verse from today's reading here:

_____
_____

DAY 222:

Mark: Chapter 16
I Corinthians: Chapter 7
Job: Chapters 15-16
Psalm 41

H: _____
What gentle whisper did you hear as you read today?

E: _____
How did the passages encourage you?

A: _____
How can you apply what you learned in your day today?

R: _____
What do you need to receive from God? His love, mercy, grace, comfort, or something else?

Write your favorite verse from today's reading here:

_____
_____

DAILY PRAYER

Lord, help me hear Your gentle whispers as I read Your Word. Encourage me as I learn more about Your heart. Help me apply what I learn and act according to Your will. And help me receive all You have for me to receive from You today. In Jesus' name, Amen.

DAY 223:

Luke: Chapter 1
I Corinthians: Chapter 8
Job: Chapters 17-18
Psalm 42

H: _____
What gentle whisper did you hear as you read today?

E: _____
How did the passages encourage you?

A: _____
How can you apply what you learned in your day today?

R: _____
What do you need to receive from God? His love, mercy, grace, comfort, or something else?

Write your favorite verse from today's reading here:

_____
_____

DAY 224:

Luke: Chapter 2
I Corinthians: Chapter 9
Job: Chapters 19-20
Psalm 43

H: _____
What gentle whisper did you hear as you read today?

E: _____
How did the passages encourage you?

A: _____
How can you apply what you learned in your day today?

R: _____
What do you need to receive from God? His love, mercy, grace, comfort, or something else?

Write your favorite verse from today's reading here:

_____
_____

DAILY PRAYER

Lord, help me hear Your gentle whispers as I read Your Word. Encourage me as I learn more about Your heart. Help me apply what I learn and act according to Your will. And help me receive all You have for me to receive from You today. In Jesus' name, Amen.

DAY 225:

Luke: Chapter 3
I Corinthians: Chapter 10
Job: Chapters 21-22
Psalm 44

H: _____
What gentle whisper did you hear as you read today?

E: _____
How did the passages encourage you?

A: _____
How can you apply what you learned in your day today?

R: _____
What do you need to receive from God? His love, mercy, grace, comfort, or something else?

Write your favorite verse from today's reading here:

_____

_____

DAY 226:

Luke: Chapter 4
I Corinthians: Chapter 11
Job: Chapters 23-24
Psalm 45

H: _____
What gentle whisper did you hear as you read today?

E: _____
How did the passages encourage you?

A: _____
How can you apply what you learned in your day today?

R: _____
What do you need to receive from God? His love, mercy, grace, comfort, or something else?

Write your favorite verse from today's reading here:

_____

_____

DAILY PRAYER

Lord, help me hear Your gentle whispers as I read Your Word. Encourage me as I learn more about Your heart. Help me apply what I learn and act according to Your will. And help me receive all You have for me to receive from You today. In Jesus' name, Amen.

DAY 227:

Luke: Chapter 5
I Corinthians: Chapter 12
Job: Chapters 25-26
Psalm 46

H: _____
What gentle whisper did you hear as you read today?

E: _____
How did the passages encourage you?

A: _____
How can you apply what you learned in your day today?

R: _____
What do you need to receive from God? His love, mercy, grace, comfort, or something else?

Write your favorite verse from today's reading here:

_____

_____

DAY 228:

Luke: Chapter 6
I Corinthians: Chapter 13
Job: Chapters 27-28
Psalm 47

H: _____
What gentle whisper did you hear as you read today?

E: _____
How did the passages encourage you?

A: _____
How can you apply what you learned in your day today?

R: _____
What do you need to receive from God? His love, mercy, grace, comfort, or something else?

Write your favorite verse from today's reading here:

_____

_____

DAILY PRAYER

Lord, help me hear Your gentle whispers as I read Your Word. Encourage me as I learn more about Your heart. Help me apply what I learn and act according to Your will. And help me receive all You have for me to receive from You today. In Jesus' name, Amen.

DAY 229:

Luke: Chapter 7
I Corinthians: Chapter 14
Job: Chapters 29-30
Psalm 48

H: _____
What gentle whisper did you hear as you read today?

E: _____
How did the passages encourage you?

A: _____
How can you apply what you learned in your day today?

R: _____
What do you need to receive from God? His love, mercy, grace, comfort, or something else?

Write your favorite verse from today's reading here:

_____

_____

DAY 230:

Luke: Chapter 8
I Corinthians: Chapter 15
Job: Chapters 31-32
Psalm 49

H: _____
What gentle whisper did you hear as you read today?

E: _____
How did the passages encourage you?

A: _____
How can you apply what you learned in your day today?

R: _____
What do you need to receive from God? His love, mercy, grace, comfort, or something else?

Write your favorite verse from today's reading here:

_____

_____

DAILY PRAYER

Lord, help me hear Your gentle whispers as I read Your Word. Encourage me as I learn more about Your heart. Help me apply what I learn and act according to Your will. And help me receive all You have for me to receive from You today. In Jesus' name, Amen.

DAY 231:

Luke: Chapter 9
I Corinthians: Chapter 16
Job: Chapters 33-34
Psalm 50

H: _____
What gentle whisper did you hear as you read today?

E: _____
How did the passages encourage you?

A: _____
How can you apply what you learned in your day today?

R: _____
What do you need to receive from God? His love, mercy, grace, comfort, or something else?

Write your favorite verse from today's reading here:

_____
_____

DAY 232:

Luke: Chapter 10
II Corinthians: Chapter 1
Job: Chapters 35-36
Psalm 51

H: _____
What gentle whisper did you hear as you read today?

E: _____
How did the passages encourage you?

A: _____
How can you apply what you learned in your day today?

R: _____
What do you need to receive from God? His love, mercy, grace, comfort, or something else?

Write your favorite verse from today's reading here:

_____
_____

DAILY PRAYER

Lord, help me hear Your gentle whispers as I read Your Word. Encourage me as I learn more about Your heart. Help me apply what I learn and act according to Your will. And help me receive all You have for me to receive from You today. In Jesus' name, Amen.

DAY 233:

Luke: Chapter 11
II Corinthians: Chapter 2
Job: Chapters 37-38
Psalm 52

H: _____
What gentle whisper did you hear as you read today?

E: _____
How did the passages encourage you?

A: _____
How can you apply what you learned in your day today?

R: _____
What do you need to receive from God? His love, mercy, grace, comfort, or something else?

Write your favorite verse from today's reading here:

_____

_____

DAY 234:

Luke: Chapter 12
II Corinthians: Chapter 3
Job: Chapters 39-40
Psalm 53

H: _____
What gentle whisper did you hear as you read today?

E: _____
How did the passages encourage you?

A: _____
How can you apply what you learned in your day today?

R: _____
What do you need to receive from God? His love, mercy, grace, comfort, or something else?

Write your favorite verse from today's reading here:

_____

_____

DAILY PRAYER

Lord, help me hear Your gentle whispers as I read Your Word. Encourage me as I learn more about Your heart. Help me apply what I learn and act according to Your will. And help me receive all You have for me to receive from You today. In Jesus' name, Amen.

DAY 235:

Luke: Chapter 13
II Corinthians: Chapter 4
Job: Chapters 41-42
Psalm 54

H: _____
What gentle whisper did you hear as you read today?

E: _____
How did the passages encourage you?

A: _____
How can you apply what you learned in your day today?

R: _____
What do you need to receive from God? His love, mercy, grace, comfort, or something else?

Write your favorite verse from today's reading here:

_____
_____

DAY 236:

Luke: Chapter 14
II Corinthians: Chapter 5
Ecclesiastes: Chapters 1-2
Psalm 55

H: _____
What gentle whisper did you hear as you read today?

E: _____
How did the passages encourage you?

A: _____
How can you apply what you learned in your day today?

R: _____
What do you need to receive from God? His love, mercy, grace, comfort, or something else?

Write your favorite verse from today's reading here:

_____
_____

DAILY PRAYER

Lord, help me hear Your gentle whispers as I read Your Word. Encourage me as I learn more about Your heart. Help me apply what I learn and act according to Your will. And help me receive all You have for me to receive from You today. In Jesus' name, Amen.

DAY 237:

Luke: Chapter 15
II Corinthians: Chapter 6
Ecclesiastes: Chapters 3-4
Psalm 56

H: _____
What gentle whisper did you hear as you read today?

E: _____
How did the passages encourage you?

A: _____
How can you apply what you learned in your day today?

R: _____
What do you need to receive from God? His love, mercy, grace, comfort, or something else?

Write your favorite verse from today's reading here:

_____

_____

DAY 238:

Luke: Chapter 16
II Corinthians: Chapter 7
Ecclesiastes: Chapters 5-6
Psalm 57

H: _____
What gentle whisper did you hear as you read today?

E: _____
How did the passages encourage you?

A: _____
How can you apply what you learned in your day today?

R: _____
What do you need to receive from God? His love, mercy, grace, comfort, or something else?

Write your favorite verse from today's reading here:

_____

_____

DAILY PRAYER

Lord, help me hear Your gentle whispers as I read Your Word. Encourage me as I learn more about Your heart. Help me apply what I learn and act according to Your will. And help me receive all You have for me to receive from You today. In Jesus' name, Amen.

DAY 239:

Luke: Chapter 17
II Corinthians: Chapter 8
Ecclesiastes: Chapters 7-8
Psalm 58

H: _____
What gentle whisper did you hear as you read today?

E: _____
How did the passages encourage you?

A: _____
How can you apply what you learned in your day today?

R: _____
What do you need to receive from God? His love, mercy, grace, comfort, or something else?

Write your favorite verse from today's reading here:

_____
_____

DAY 240:

Luke: Chapter 18
II Corinthians: Chapter 9
Ecclesiastes: Chapters 9-10
Psalm 59

H: _____
What gentle whisper did you hear as you read today?

E: _____
How did the passages encourage you?

A: _____
How can you apply what you learned in your day today?

R: _____
What do you need to receive from God? His love, mercy, grace, comfort, or something else?

Write your favorite verse from today's reading here:

_____
_____

DAILY PRAYER

Lord, help me hear Your gentle whispers as I read Your Word. Encourage me as I learn more about Your heart. Help me apply what I learn and act according to Your will. And help me receive all You have for me to receive from You today. In Jesus' name, Amen.

DAY 241:

Luke: Chapter 19
II Corinthians: Chapter 10
Ecclesiastes: Chapters 11-12
Psalm 60

H: _____
What gentle whisper did you hear as you read today?

E: _____
How did the passages encourage you?

A: _____
How can you apply what you learned in your day today?

R: _____
What do you need to receive from God? His love, mercy, grace, comfort, or something else?

Write your favorite verse from today's reading here:

_____

_____

DAY 242:

Luke: Chapter 20
II Corinthians: Chapter 11
Song of Solomon: Chapters 1-2
Psalm 61

H: _____
What gentle whisper did you hear as you read today?

E: _____
How did the passages encourage you?

A: _____
How can you apply what you learned in your day today?

R: _____
What do you need to receive from God? His love, mercy, grace, comfort, or something else?

Write your favorite verse from today's reading here:

_____

_____

DAILY PRAYER

Lord, help me hear Your gentle whispers as I read Your Word. Encourage me as I learn more about Your heart. Help me apply what I learn and act according to Your will. And help me receive all You have for me to receive from You today. In Jesus' name, Amen.

DAY 243:

Luke: Chapter 21
II Corinthians: Chapter 12
Song of Solomon:
Chapters 3-4
Psalm 62

H: _____
What gentle whisper did you hear as you read today?

E: _____
How did the passages encourage you?

A: _____
How can you apply what you learned in your day today?

R: _____
What do you need to receive from God? His love, mercy, grace, comfort, or something else?

Write your favorite verse from today's reading here:

_____

_____

DAY 244:

Luke: Chapter 22
II Corinthians: Chapter 13
Song of Solomon:
Chapters 5-6
Psalm 63

H: _____
What gentle whisper did you hear as you read today?

E: _____
How did the passages encourage you?

A: _____
How can you apply what you learned in your day today?

R: _____
What do you need to receive from God? His love, mercy, grace, comfort, or something else?

Write your favorite verse from today's reading here:

_____

_____

DAILY PRAYER

Lord, help me hear Your gentle whispers as I read Your Word. Encourage me as I learn more about Your heart. Help me apply what I learn and act according to Your will. And help me receive all You have for me to receive from You today. In Jesus' name, Amen.

DAY 245:

Luke: Chapter 23
Galatians: Chapter 1
Song of Solomon:
Chapters 7-8
Psalm 64

H: _____
What gentle whisper did you hear as you read today?

E: _____
How did the passages encourage you?

A: _____
How can you apply what you learned in your day today?

R: _____
What do you need to receive from God? His love, mercy, grace, comfort, or something else?

Write your favorite verse from today's reading here:

_____

_____

DAY 246:

Luke: Chapter 24
Galatians: Chapter 2
Isaiah: Chapters 1-2
Psalm 65

H: _____
What gentle whisper did you hear as you read today?

E: _____
How did the passages encourage you?

A: _____
How can you apply what you learned in your day today?

R: _____
What do you need to receive from God? His love, mercy, grace, comfort, or something else?

Write your favorite verse from today's reading here:

_____

_____

DAILY PRAYER

Lord, help me hear Your gentle whispers as I read Your Word. Encourage me as I learn more about Your heart. Help me apply what I learn and act according to Your will. And help me receive all You have for me to receive from You today. In Jesus' name, Amen.

DAY 247:

John: Chapter 1
Galatians: Chapter 3
Isaiah: Chapters 3-4
Psalm 66

H: _____
What gentle whisper did you hear as you read today?

E: _____
How did the passages encourage you?

A: _____
How can you apply what you learned in your day today?

R: _____
What do you need to receive from God? His love, mercy, grace, comfort, or something else?

Write your favorite verse from today's reading here:

_____

_____

DAY 248:

John: Chapter 2
Galatians: Chapter 4
Isaiah: Chapters 5-6
Psalm 67

H: _____
What gentle whisper did you hear as you read today?

E: _____
How did the passages encourage you?

A: _____
How can you apply what you learned in your day today?

R: _____
What do you need to receive from God? His love, mercy, grace, comfort, or something else?

Write your favorite verse from today's reading here:

_____

_____

DAILY PRAYER

Lord, help me hear Your gentle whispers as I read Your Word. Encourage me as I learn more about Your heart. Help me apply what I learn and act according to Your will. And help me receive all You have for me to receive from You today. In Jesus' name, Amen.

DAY 249:

John: Chapter 3
Galatians: Chapter 5
Isaiah: Chapters 7-8
Psalm 68

H: _____
What gentle whisper did you hear as you read today?

E: _____
How did the passages encourage you?

A: _____
How can you apply what you learned in your day today?

R: _____
What do you need to receive from God? His love, mercy, grace, comfort, or something else?

Write your favorite verse from today's reading here:

_____

_____

DAY 250:

John: Chapter 4
Galatians: Chapter 6
Isaiah: Chapters 9-10
Psalm 69

H: _____
What gentle whisper did you hear as you read today?

E: _____
How did the passages encourage you?

A: _____
How can you apply what you learned in your day today?

R: _____
What do you need to receive from God? His love, mercy, grace, comfort, or something else?

Write your favorite verse from today's reading here:

_____

_____

DAILY PRAYER

Lord, help me hear Your gentle whispers as I read Your Word. Encourage me as I learn more about Your heart. Help me apply what I learn and act according to Your will. And help me receive all You have for me to receive from You today. In Jesus' name, Amen.

DAY 251:

John: Chapter 5
Ephesians: Chapter 1
Isaiah: Chapters 11-12
Psalm 70

H: _____
What gentle whisper did you hear as you read today?

E: _____
How did the passages encourage you?

A: _____
How can you apply what you learned in your day today?

R: _____
What do you need to receive from God? His love, mercy, grace, comfort, or something else?

Write your favorite verse from today's reading here:

_____

_____

DAY 252:

John: Chapter 6
Ephesians: Chapter 2
Isaiah: Chapters 13-14
Psalm 71

H: _____
What gentle whisper did you hear as you read today?

E: _____
How did the passages encourage you?

A: _____
How can you apply what you learned in your day today?

R: _____
What do you need to receive from God? His love, mercy, grace, comfort, or something else?

Write your favorite verse from today's reading here:

_____

_____

DAILY PRAYER

Lord, help me hear Your gentle whispers as I read Your Word. Encourage me as I learn more about Your heart. Help me apply what I learn and act according to Your will. And help me receive all You have for me to receive from You today. In Jesus' name, Amen.

DAY 253:

John: Chapter 7
Ephesians: Chapter 3
Isaiah: Chapters 15-16
Psalm 72

H: _____
What gentle whisper did you hear as you read today?

E: _____
How did the passages encourage you?

A: _____
How can you apply what you learned in your day today?

R: _____
What do you need to receive from God? His love, mercy, grace, comfort, or something else?

Write your favorite verse from today's reading here:

_____

_____

DAY 254:

John: Chapter 8
Ephesians: Chapter 4
Isaiah: Chapters 17-18
Psalm 73

H: _____
What gentle whisper did you hear as you read today?

E: _____
How did the passages encourage you?

A: _____
How can you apply what you learned in your day today?

R: _____
What do you need to receive from God? His love, mercy, grace, comfort, or something else?

Write your favorite verse from today's reading here:

_____

_____

DAILY PRAYER

Lord, help me hear Your gentle whispers as I read Your Word. Encourage me as I learn more about Your heart. Help me apply what I learn and act according to Your will. And help me receive all You have for me to receive from You today. In Jesus' name, Amen.

DAY 255:

John: Chapter 9
Ephesians: Chapter 5
Isaiah: Chapters 19-20
Psalm 74

H: _____
What gentle whisper did you hear as you read today?

E: _____
How did the passages encourage you?

A: _____
How can you apply what you learned in your day today?

R: _____
What do you need to receive from God? His love, mercy, grace, comfort, or something else?

Write your favorite verse from today's reading here:

_____
_____

DAY 256:

John: Chapter 10
Ephesians: Chapter 6
Isaiah: Chapters 21-22
Psalm 75

H: _____
What gentle whisper did you hear as you read today?

E: _____
How did the passages encourage you?

A: _____
How can you apply what you learned in your day today?

R: _____
What do you need to receive from God? His love, mercy, grace, comfort, or something else?

Write your favorite verse from today's reading here:

_____
_____

DAILY PRAYER

Lord, help me hear Your gentle whispers as I read Your Word. Encourage me as I learn more about Your heart. Help me apply what I learn and act according to Your will. And help me receive all You have for me to receive from You today. In Jesus' name, Amen.

DAY 257:

John: Chapter 11
Philippians: Chapter 1
Isaiah: Chapters 23-24
Psalm 76

H: _____
What gentle whisper did you hear as you read today?

E: _____
How did the passages encourage you?

A: _____
How can you apply what you learned in your day today?

R: _____
What do you need to receive from God? His love, mercy, grace, comfort, or something else?

Write your favorite verse from today's reading here:

_____

_____

DAY 258:

John: Chapter 12
Philippians: Chapter 2
Isaiah: Chapters 25-26
Psalm 77

H: _____
What gentle whisper did you hear as you read today?

E: _____
How did the passages encourage you?

A: _____
How can you apply what you learned in your day today?

R: _____
What do you need to receive from God? His love, mercy, grace, comfort, or something else?

Write your favorite verse from today's reading here:

_____

_____

DAILY PRAYER

Lord, help me hear Your gentle whispers as I read Your Word. Encourage me as I learn more about Your heart. Help me apply what I learn and act according to Your will. And help me receive all You have for me to receive from You today. In Jesus' name, Amen.

DAY 259:

John: Chapter 13
Philippians: Chapter 3
Isaiah: Chapters 27-28
Psalm 78

H: _____
What gentle whisper did you hear as you read today?

E: _____
How did the passages encourage you?

A: _____
How can you apply what you learned in your day today?

R: _____
What do you need to receive from God? His love, mercy, grace, comfort, or something else?

Write your favorite verse from today's reading here:

_____

_____

DAY 260:

John: Chapter 14
Philippians: Chapter 4
Isaiah: Chapters 29-30
Psalm 79

H: _____
What gentle whisper did you hear as you read today?

E: _____
How did the passages encourage you?

A: _____
How can you apply what you learned in your day today?

R: _____
What do you need to receive from God? His love, mercy, grace, comfort, or something else?

Write your favorite verse from today's reading here:

_____

_____

DAILY PRAYER

Lord, help me hear Your gentle whispers as I read Your Word. Encourage me as I learn more about Your heart. Help me apply what I learn and act according to Your will. And help me receive all You have for me to receive from You today. In Jesus' name, Amen.

DAY 261:

John: Chapter 15
Colossians: Chapter 1
Isaiah: Chapters 31-32
Psalm 80

H: _____
What gentle whisper did you hear as you read today?

E: _____
How did the passages encourage you?

A: _____
How can you apply what you learned in your day today?

R: _____
What do you need to receive from God? His love, mercy, grace, comfort, or something else?

Write your favorite verse from today's reading here:

_____
_____

DAY 262:

John: Chapter 16
Colossians: Chapter 2
Isaiah: Chapters 33-34
Psalm 81

H: _____
What gentle whisper did you hear as you read today?

E: _____
How did the passages encourage you?

A: _____
How can you apply what you learned in your day today?

R: _____
What do you need to receive from God? His love, mercy, grace, comfort, or something else?

Write your favorite verse from today's reading here:

_____
_____

DAILY PRAYER

Lord, help me hear Your gentle whispers as I read Your Word. Encourage me as I learn more about Your heart. Help me apply what I learn and act according to Your will. And help me receive all You have for me to receive from You today. In Jesus' name, Amen.

DAY 263:

John: Chapter 17
Colossians: Chapter 3
Isaiah: Chapters 35-36
Psalm 82

H: _____
What gentle whisper did you hear as you read today?

E: _____
How did the passages encourage you?

A: _____
How can you apply what you learned in your day today?

R: _____
What do you need to receive from God? His love, mercy, grace, comfort, or something else?

Write your favorite verse from today's reading here:

_____
_____

DAY 264:

John: Chapter 18
Colossians: Chapter 4
Isaiah: Chapters 37-38
Psalm 83

H: _____
What gentle whisper did you hear as you read today?

E: _____
How did the passages encourage you?

A: _____
How can you apply what you learned in your day today?

R: _____
What do you need to receive from God? His love, mercy, grace, comfort, or something else?

Write your favorite verse from today's reading here:

_____
_____

DAILY PRAYER

Lord, help me hear Your gentle whispers as I read Your Word. Encourage me as I learn more about Your heart. Help me apply what I learn and act according to Your will. And help me receive all You have for me to receive from You today. In Jesus' name, Amen.

DAY 265:

John: Chapter 19
I Thessalonians:
Chapter 1
Isaiah: Chapters 39-40
Psalm 84

H: _____
What gentle whisper did you hear as you read today?

E: _____
How did the passages encourage you?

A: _____
How can you apply what you learned in your day today?

R: _____
What do you need to receive from God? His love, mercy, grace, comfort, or something else?

Write your favorite verse from today's reading here:

_____

_____

DAY 266:

John: Chapter 20
I Thessalonians:
Chapter 2
Isaiah: Chapters 41-42
Psalm 85

H: _____
What gentle whisper did you hear as you read today?

E: _____
How did the passages encourage you?

A: _____
How can you apply what you learned in your day today?

R: _____
What do you need to receive from God? His love, mercy, grace, comfort, or something else?

Write your favorite verse from today's reading here:

_____

_____

DAILY PRAYER

Lord, help me hear Your gentle whispers as I read Your Word. Encourage me as I learn more about Your heart. Help me apply what I learn and act according to Your will. And help me receive all You have for me to receive from You today. In Jesus' name, Amen.

DAY 267:

John: Chapter 21
I Thessalonians: Chapter 3
Isaiah: Chapters 43-44
Psalm 86

H: _____
What gentle whisper did you hear as you read today?

E: _____
How did the passages encourage you?

A: _____
How can you apply what you learned in your day today?

R: _____
What do you need to receive from God? His love, mercy, grace, comfort, or something else?

Write your favorite verse from today's reading here:

_____

_____

DAY 268:

Matthew: Chapter 1
I Thessalonians: Chapter 4
Isaiah: Chapters 45-46
Psalm 87

H: _____
What gentle whisper did you hear as you read today?

E: _____
How did the passages encourage you?

A: _____
How can you apply what you learned in your day today?

R: _____
What do you need to receive from God? His love, mercy, grace, comfort, or something else?

Write your favorite verse from today's reading here:

_____

_____

DAILY PRAYER

Lord, help me hear Your gentle whispers as I read Your Word. Encourage me as I learn more about Your heart. Help me apply what I learn and act according to Your will. And help me receive all You have for me to receive from You today. In Jesus' name, Amen.

DAY 269:

Matthew: Chapter 2
I Thessalonians:
Chapter 5
Isaiah: Chapters 47-48
Psalm 88

H: _____
What gentle whisper did you hear as you read today?

E: _____
How did the passages encourage you?

A: _____
How can you apply what you learned in your day today?

R: _____
What do you need to receive from God? His love, mercy, grace, comfort, or something else?

Write your favorite verse from today's reading here:

_____
_____

DAY 270:

Matthew: Chapter 3
II Thessalonians:
Chapter 1
Isaiah: Chapters 49-50
Psalm 89

H: _____
What gentle whisper did you hear as you read today?

E: _____
How did the passages encourage you?

A: _____
How can you apply what you learned in your day today?

R: _____
What do you need to receive from God? His love, mercy, grace, comfort, or something else?

Write your favorite verse from today's reading here:

_____
_____

DAILY PRAYER

Lord, help me hear Your gentle whispers as I read Your Word. Encourage me as I learn more about Your heart. Help me apply what I learn and act according to Your will. And help me receive all You have for me to receive from You today. In Jesus' name, Amen.

DAY 271:

Matthew: Chapter 4
II Thessalonians:
Chapter 2
Isaiah: Chapters 51-52
Psalm 90

H: _____
What gentle whisper did you hear as you read today?

E: _____
How did the passages encourage you?

A: _____
How can you apply what you learned in your day today?

R: _____
What do you need to receive from God? His love, mercy, grace, comfort, or something else?

Write your favorite verse from today's reading here:

_____
_____

DAY 272:

Matthew: Chapter 5
II Thessalonians:
Chapter 3
Isaiah: Chapters 53-54
Psalm 91

H: _____
What gentle whisper did you hear as you read today?

E: _____
How did the passages encourage you?

A: _____
How can you apply what you learned in your day today?

R: _____
What do you need to receive from God? His love, mercy, grace, comfort, or something else?

Write your favorite verse from today's reading here:

_____
_____

DAILY PRAYER

Lord, help me hear Your gentle whispers as I read Your Word. Encourage me as I learn more about Your heart. Help me apply what I learn and act according to Your will. And help me receive all You have for me to receive from You today. In Jesus' name, Amen.

DAY 273:

Matthew: Chapter 6
I Timothy: Chapter 1
Isaiah: Chapters 55-56
Psalm 92

H: _____
What gentle whisper did you hear as you read today?

E: _____
How did the passages encourage you?

A: _____
How can you apply what you learned in your day today?

R: _____
What do you need to receive from God? His love, mercy, grace, comfort, or something else?

Write your favorite verse from today's reading here:

_____
_____

DAY 274:

Matthew: Chapter 7
I Timothy: Chapter 2
Isaiah: Chapters 57-58
Psalm 93

H: _____
What gentle whisper did you hear as you read today?

E: _____
How did the passages encourage you?

A: _____
How can you apply what you learned in your day today?

R: _____
What do you need to receive from God? His love, mercy, grace, comfort, or something else?

Write your favorite verse from today's reading here:

_____
_____

DAILY PRAYER

Lord, help me hear Your gentle whispers as I read Your Word. Encourage me as I learn more about Your heart. Help me apply what I learn and act according to Your will. And help me receive all You have for me to receive from You today. In Jesus' name, Amen.

DAY 275:

Matthew: Chapter 8
I Timothy: Chapter 3
Isaiah: Chapters 59-60
Psalm 94

H: _____
What gentle whisper did you hear as you read today?

E: _____
How did the passages encourage you?

A: _____
How can you apply what you learned in your day today?

R: _____
What do you need to receive from God? His love, mercy, grace, comfort, or something else?

Write your favorite verse from today's reading here:

_____
_____

DAY 276:

Matthew: Chapter 9
I Timothy: Chapter 4
Isaiah: Chapters 61-62
Psalm 95

H: _____
What gentle whisper did you hear as you read today?

E: _____
How did the passages encourage you?

A: _____
How can you apply what you learned in your day today?

R: _____
What do you need to receive from God? His love, mercy, grace, comfort, or something else?

Write your favorite verse from today's reading here:

_____
_____

DAILY PRAYER

Lord, help me hear Your gentle whispers as I read Your Word. Encourage me as I learn more about Your heart. Help me apply what I learn and act according to Your will. And help me receive all You have for me to receive from You today. In Jesus' name, Amen.

DAY 277:

Matthew: Chapter 10
I Timothy: Chapter 5
Isaiah: Chapters 63-64
Psalm 96

H: _____
What gentle whisper did you hear as you read today?

E: _____
How did the passages encourage you?

A: _____
How can you apply what you learned in your day today?

R: _____
What do you need to receive from God? His love, mercy, grace, comfort, or something else?

Write your favorite verse from today's reading here:

_____
_____

DAY 278:

Matthew: Chapter 11
I Timothy: Chapter 6
Isaiah: Chapters 65-66
Psalm 97

H: _____
What gentle whisper did you hear as you read today?

E: _____
How did the passages encourage you?

A: _____
How can you apply what you learned in your day today?

R: _____
What do you need to receive from God? His love, mercy, grace, comfort, or something else?

Write your favorite verse from today's reading here:

_____
_____

DAILY PRAYER

Lord, help me hear Your gentle whispers as I read Your Word. Encourage me as I learn more about Your heart. Help me apply what I learn and act according to Your will. And help me receive all You have for me to receive from You today. In Jesus' name, Amen.

DAY 279:

Matthew: Chapter 12
II Timothy: Chapter 1
Jeremiah: Chapters 1-2
Psalm 98

H: _____
What gentle whisper did you hear as you read today?

E: _____
How did the passages encourage you?

A: _____
How can you apply what you learned in your day today?

R: _____
What do you need to receive from God? His love, mercy, grace, comfort, or something else?

Write your favorite verse from today's reading here:

_____

_____

DAY 280:

Matthew: Chapter 13
II Timothy: Chapter 2
Jeremiah: Chapters 3-4
Psalm 99

H: _____
What gentle whisper did you hear as you read today?

E: _____
How did the passages encourage you?

A: _____
How can you apply what you learned in your day today?

R: _____
What do you need to receive from God? His love, mercy, grace, comfort, or something else?

Write your favorite verse from today's reading here:

_____

_____

DAILY PRAYER

Lord, help me hear Your gentle whispers as I read Your Word. Encourage me as I learn more about Your heart. Help me apply what I learn and act according to Your will. And help me receive all You have for me to receive from You today. In Jesus' name, Amen.

DAY 281:

Matthew: Chapter 14
II Timothy: Chapter 3
Jeremiah: Chapters 5-6
Psalm 100

H: _____
What gentle whisper did you hear as you read today?

E: _____
How did the passages encourage you?

A: _____
How can you apply what you learned in your day today?

R: _____
What do you need to receive from God? His love, mercy, grace, comfort, or something else?

Write your favorite verse from today's reading here:

_____

_____

DAY 282:

Matthew: Chapter 15
II Timothy: Chapter 4
Jeremiah: Chapters 7-8
Psalm 101

H: _____
What gentle whisper did you hear as you read today?

E: _____
How did the passages encourage you?

A: _____
How can you apply what you learned in your day today?

R: _____
What do you need to receive from God? His love, mercy, grace, comfort, or something else?

Write your favorite verse from today's reading here:

_____

_____

DAILY PRAYER

Lord, help me hear Your gentle whispers as I read Your Word. Encourage me as I learn more about Your heart. Help me apply what I learn and act according to Your will. And help me receive all You have for me to receive from You today. In Jesus' name, Amen.

DAY 283:

Matthew: Chapter 16
Titus: Chapter 1
Jeremiah: Chapters 9-10
Psalm 102

H: _____
What gentle whisper did you hear as you read today?

E: _____
How did the passages encourage you?

A: _____
How can you apply what you learned in your day today?

R: _____
What do you need to receive from God? His love, mercy, grace, comfort, or something else?

Write your favorite verse from today's reading here:

_____

_____

DAY 284:

Matthew: Chapter 17
Titus: Chapter 2
Jeremiah: Chapters 11-12
Psalm 103

H: _____
What gentle whisper did you hear as you read today?

E: _____
How did the passages encourage you?

A: _____
How can you apply what you learned in your day today?

R: _____
What do you need to receive from God? His love, mercy, grace, comfort, or something else?

Write your favorite verse from today's reading here:

_____

_____

DAILY PRAYER

Lord, help me hear Your gentle whispers as I read Your Word. Encourage me as I learn more about Your heart. Help me apply what I learn and act according to Your will. And help me receive all You have for me to receive from You today. In Jesus' name, Amen.

DAY 285:

Matthew: Chapter 18
Titus: Chapter 3
Jeremiah: Chapters 13-14
Psalm 104

H: _____
What gentle whisper did you hear as you read today?

E: _____
How did the passages encourage you?

A: _____
How can you apply what you learned in your day today?

R: _____
What do you need to receive from God? His love, mercy, grace, comfort, or something else?

Write your favorite verse from today's reading here:

_____

_____

DAY 286:

Matthew: Chapter 19
Philemon: Chapter 1
Jeremiah: Chapters 15-16
Psalm 105

H: _____
What gentle whisper did you hear as you read today?

E: _____
How did the passages encourage you?

A: _____
How can you apply what you learned in your day today?

R: _____
What do you need to receive from God? His love, mercy, grace, comfort, or something else?

Write your favorite verse from today's reading here:

_____

_____

DAILY PRAYER

Lord, help me hear Your gentle whispers as I read Your Word. Encourage me as I learn more about Your heart. Help me apply what I learn and act according to Your will. And help me receive all You have for me to receive from You today. In Jesus' name, Amen.

DAY 287:

Matthew: Chapter 20
Hebrews: Chapter 1
Jeremiah: Chapters 17-18
Psalm 106

H: _____
What gentle whisper did you hear as you read today?

E: _____
How did the passages encourage you?

A: _____
How can you apply what you learned in your day today?

R: _____
What do you need to receive from God? His love, mercy, grace, comfort, or something else?

Write your favorite verse from today's reading here:

_____

_____

DAY 288:

Matthew: Chapter 21
Hebrews: Chapter 2
Jeremiah: Chapters 19-20
Psalm 107

H: _____
What gentle whisper did you hear as you read today?

E: _____
How did the passages encourage you?

A: _____
How can you apply what you learned in your day today?

R: _____
What do you need to receive from God? His love, mercy, grace, comfort, or something else?

Write your favorite verse from today's reading here:

_____

_____

DAILY PRAYER

Lord, help me hear Your gentle whispers as I read Your Word. Encourage me as I learn more about Your heart. Help me apply what I learn and act according to Your will. And help me receive all You have for me to receive from You today. In Jesus' name, Amen.

DAY 289:

Matthew: Chapter 22
Hebrews: Chapter 3
Jeremiah: Chapters 21-22
Psalm 108

H: _____
What gentle whisper did you hear as you read today?

E: _____
How did the passages encourage you?

A: _____
How can you apply what you learned in your day today?

R: _____
What do you need to receive from God? His love, mercy, grace, comfort, or something else?

Write your favorite verse from today's reading here:

_____

_____

DAY 290:

Matthew: Chapter 23
Hebrews: Chapter 4
Jeremiah: Chapters 23-24
Psalm 109

H: _____
What gentle whisper did you hear as you read today?

E: _____
How did the passages encourage you?

A: _____
How can you apply what you learned in your day today?

R: _____
What do you need to receive from God? His love, mercy, grace, comfort, or something else?

Write your favorite verse from today's reading here:

_____

_____

DAILY PRAYER

Lord, help me hear Your gentle whispers as I read Your Word. Encourage me as I learn more about Your heart. Help me apply what I learn and act according to Your will. And help me receive all You have for me to receive from You today. In Jesus' name, Amen.

DAY 291:

Matthew: Chapter 24
Hebrews: Chapter 5
Jeremiah: Chapters 25-26
Psalm 110

H: _____
What gentle whisper did you hear as you read today?

E: _____
How did the passages encourage you?

A: _____
How can you apply what you learned in your day today?

R: _____
What do you need to receive from God? His love, mercy, grace, comfort, or something else?

Write your favorite verse from today's reading here:

_____

_____

DAY 292:

Matthew: Chapter 25
Hebrews: Chapter 6
Jeremiah: Chapters 27-28
Psalm 111

H: _____
What gentle whisper did you hear as you read today?

E: _____
How did the passages encourage you?

A: _____
How can you apply what you learned in your day today?

R: _____
What do you need to receive from God? His love, mercy, grace, comfort, or something else?

Write your favorite verse from today's reading here:

_____

_____

DAILY PRAYER

Lord, help me hear Your gentle whispers as I read Your Word. Encourage me as I learn more about Your heart. Help me apply what I learn and act according to Your will. And help me receive all You have for me to receive from You today. In Jesus' name, Amen.

DAY 293:

Matthew: Chapter 26
Hebrews: Chapter 7
Jeremiah: Chapters 29-30
Psalm 112

H: _____
What gentle whisper did you hear as you read today?

E: _____
How did the passages encourage you?

A: _____
How can you apply what you learned in your day today?

R: _____
What do you need to receive from God? His love, mercy, grace, comfort, or something else?

Write your favorite verse from today's reading here:

_____

_____

DAY 294:

Matthew: Chapter 27
Hebrews: Chapter 8
Jeremiah: Chapters 31-32
Psalm 113

H: _____
What gentle whisper did you hear as you read today?

E: _____
How did the passages encourage you?

A: _____
How can you apply what you learned in your day today?

R: _____
What do you need to receive from God? His love, mercy, grace, comfort, or something else?

Write your favorite verse from today's reading here:

_____

_____

DAILY PRAYER

Lord, help me hear Your gentle whispers as I read Your Word. Encourage me as I learn more about Your heart. Help me apply what I learn and act according to Your will. And help me receive all You have for me to receive from You today. In Jesus' name, Amen.

DAY 295:

Matthew: Chapter 28
Hebrews: Chapter 9
Jeremiah: Chapters 33-34
Psalm 114

H: _____
What gentle whisper did you hear as you read today?

E: _____
How did the passages encourage you?

A: _____
How can you apply what you learned in your day today?

R: _____
What do you need to receive from God? His love, mercy, grace, comfort, or something else?

.Write your favorite verse from today's reading here:

_____
_____

DAY 296:

Mark: Chapter 1
Hebrews: Chapter 10
Jeremiah: Chapters 35-36
Psalm 115

H: _____
What gentle whisper did you hear as you read today?

E: _____
How did the passages encourage you?

A: _____
How can you apply what you learned in your day today?

R: _____
What do you need to receive from God? His love, mercy, grace, comfort, or something else?

Write your favorite verse from today's reading here:

_____
_____

DAILY PRAYER

Lord, help me hear Your gentle whispers as I read Your Word. Encourage me as I learn more about Your heart. Help me apply what I learn and act according to Your will. And help me receive all You have for me to receive from You today. In Jesus' name, Amen.

DAY 297:

Mark: Chapter 2
Hebrews: Chapter 11
Jeremiah: Chapters 37-38
Psalm 116

H: _____
What gentle whisper did you hear as you read today?

E: _____
How did the passages encourage you?

A: _____
How can you apply what you learned in your day today?

R: _____
What do you need to receive from God? His love, mercy, grace, comfort, or something else?

Write your favorite verse from today's reading here:

_____
_____

DAY 298:

Mark: Chapter 3
Hebrews: Chapter 12
Jeremiah: Chapters 39-40
Psalm 117

H: _____
What gentle whisper did you hear as you read today?

E: _____
How did the passages encourage you?

A: _____
How can you apply what you learned in your day today?

R: _____
What do you need to receive from God? His love, mercy, grace, comfort, or something else?

Write your favorite verse from today's reading here:

_____
_____

DAILY PRAYER

Lord, help me hear Your gentle whispers as I read Your Word. Encourage me as I learn more about Your heart. Help me apply what I learn and act according to Your will. And help me receive all You have for me to receive from You today. In Jesus' name, Amen.

DAY 299:

Mark: Chapter 4
Hebrews: Chapter 13
Jeremiah: Chapters 41-42
Psalm 118

H: _____
What gentle whisper did you hear as you read today?

E: _____
How did the passages encourage you?

A: _____
How can you apply what you learned in your day today?

R: _____
What do you need to receive from God? His love, mercy, grace, comfort, or something else?

Write your favorite verse from today's reading here:

_____

_____

DAY 300:

Mark: Chapter 5
James: Chapter 1
Jeremiah: Chapters 43-44
Psalm 119

H: _____
What gentle whisper did you hear as you read today?

E: _____
How did the passages encourage you?

A: _____
How can you apply what you learned in your day today?

R: _____
What do you need to receive from God? His love, mercy, grace, comfort, or something else?

Write your favorite verse from today's reading here:

_____

_____

DAILY PRAYER

Lord, help me hear Your gentle whispers as I read Your Word. Encourage me as I learn more about Your heart. Help me apply what I learn and act according to Your will. And help me receive all You have for me to receive from You today. In Jesus' name, Amen.

DAY 301:

Mark: Chapter 6
James: Chapter 2
Jeremiah: Chapters 45-46
Psalm 120

H: _____
What gentle whisper did you hear as you read today?

E: _____
How did the passages encourage you?

A: _____
How can you apply what you learned in your day today?

R: _____
What do you need to receive from God? His love, mercy, grace, comfort, or something else?

Write your favorite verse from today's reading here:

_____

_____

DAY 302:

Mark: Chapter 7
James: Chapter 3
Jeremiah: Chapters 47-48
Psalm 121

H: _____
What gentle whisper did you hear as you read today?

E: _____
How did the passages encourage you?

A: _____
How can you apply what you learned in your day today?

R: _____
What do you need to receive from God? His love, mercy, grace, comfort, or something else?

Write your favorite verse from today's reading here:

_____

_____

DAILY PRAYER

Lord, help me hear Your gentle whispers as I read Your Word. Encourage me as I learn more about Your heart. Help me apply what I learn and act according to Your will. And help me receive all You have for me to receive from You today. In Jesus' name, Amen.

DAY 303:

Mark: Chapter 8
James: Chapter 4
Jeremiah: Chapters 49-50
Psalm 122

H: _____
What gentle whisper did you hear as you read today?

E: _____
How did the passages encourage you?

A: _____
How can you apply what you learned in your day today?

R: _____
What do you need to receive from God? His love, mercy, grace, comfort, or something else?

Write your favorite verse from today's reading here:

_____
_____

DAY 304:

Mark: Chapter 9
James: Chapter 5
Jeremiah: Chapters 51-52
Psalm 123

H: _____
What gentle whisper did you hear as you read today?

E: _____
How did the passages encourage you?

A: _____
How can you apply what you learned in your day today?

R: _____
What do you need to receive from God? His love, mercy, grace, comfort, or something else?

Write your favorite verse from today's reading here:

_____
_____

DAILY PRAYER

Lord, help me hear Your gentle whispers as I read Your Word. Encourage me as I learn more about Your heart. Help me apply what I learn and act according to Your will. And help me receive all You have for me to receive from You today. In Jesus' name, Amen.

DAY 305:

Mark: Chapter 10
I Peter: Chapter 1
Lamentation: Chapters 1-2
Psalm 124

H: _____
What gentle whisper did you hear as you read today?

E: _____
How did the passages encourage you?

A: _____
How can you apply what you learned in your day today?

R: _____
What do you need to receive from God? His love, mercy, grace, comfort, or something else?

Write your favorite verse from today's reading here:

_____

_____

DAY 306:

Mark: Chapter 11
I Peter: Chapter 2
Lamentation: Chapters 3-5
Psalm 125

H: _____
What gentle whisper did you hear as you read today?

E: _____
How did the passages encourage you?

A: _____
How can you apply what you learned in your day today?

R: _____
What do you need to receive from God? His love, mercy, grace, comfort, or something else?

Write your favorite verse from today's reading here:

_____

_____

DAILY PRAYER

Lord, help me hear Your gentle whispers as I read Your Word. Encourage me as I learn more about Your heart. Help me apply what I learn and act according to Your will. And help me receive all You have for me to receive from You today. In Jesus' name, Amen.

DAY 307:

Mark: Chapter 12
I Peter: Chapter 3
Ezekiel: Chapters 1-2
Psalm 126

H: _____
What gentle whisper did you hear as you read today?

E: _____
How did the passages encourage you?

A: _____
How can you apply what you learned in your day today?

R: _____
What do you need to receive from God? His love, mercy, grace, comfort, or something else?

Write your favorite verse from today's reading here:

_____

_____

DAY 308:

Mark: Chapter 13
I Peter: Chapter 4
Ezekiel: Chapters 3-4
Psalm 127

H: _____
What gentle whisper did you hear as you read today?

E: _____
How did the passages encourage you?

A: _____
How can you apply what you learned in your day today?

R: _____
What do you need to receive from God? His love, mercy, grace, comfort, or something else?

Write your favorite verse from today's reading here:

_____

_____

DAILY PRAYER

Lord, help me hear Your gentle whispers as I read Your Word. Encourage me as I learn more about Your heart. Help me apply what I learn and act according to Your will. And help me receive all You have for me to receive from You today. In Jesus' name, Amen.

DAY 309:

Mark: Chapter 14
I Peter: Chapter 5
Ezekiel: Chapters 5-6
Psalm 128

H: _____
What gentle whisper did you hear as you read today?

E: _____
How did the passages encourage you?

A: _____
How can you apply what you learned in your day today?

R: _____
What do you need to receive from God? His love, mercy, grace, comfort, or something else?

Write your favorite verse from today's reading here:

_____

_____

DAY 310:

Mark: Chapter 15
II Peter: Chapter 1
Ezekiel: Chapters 7-8
Psalm 129

H: _____
What gentle whisper did you hear as you read today?

E: _____
How did the passages encourage you?

A: _____
How can you apply what you learned in your day today?

R: _____
What do you need to receive from God? His love, mercy, grace, comfort, or something else?

Write your favorite verse from today's reading here:

_____

_____

DAILY PRAYER

Lord, help me hear Your gentle whispers as I read Your Word. Encourage me as I learn more about Your heart. Help me apply what I learn and act according to Your will. And help me receive all You have for me to receive from You today. In Jesus' name, Amen.

DAY 311:

Mark: Chapter 16
II Peter: Chapter 2
Ezekiel: Chapters 9-10
Psalm 130

H: _____
What gentle whisper did you hear as you read today?

E: _____
How did the passages encourage you?

A: _____
How can you apply what you learned in your day today?

R: _____
What do you need to receive from God? His love, mercy, grace, comfort, or something else?

Write your favorite verse from today's reading here:

_____
_____

DAY 312:

Luke: Chapter 1
II Peter: Chapter 3
Ezekiel: Chapters 11-12
Psalm 131

H: _____
What gentle whisper did you hear as you read today?

E: _____
How did the passages encourage you?

A: _____
How can you apply what you learned in your day today?

R: _____
What do you need to receive from God? His love, mercy, grace, comfort, or something else?

Write your favorite verse from today's reading here:

_____
_____

DAILY PRAYER

Lord, help me hear Your gentle whispers as I read Your Word. Encourage me as I learn more about Your heart. Help me apply what I learn and act according to Your will. And help me receive all You have for me to receive from You today. In Jesus' name, Amen.

DAY 313:

Luke: Chapter 2
I John: Chapter 1
Ezekiel: Chapters 13-14
Psalm 132

H: _____
What gentle whisper did you hear as you read today?

E: _____
How did the passages encourage you?

A: _____
How can you apply what you learned in your day today?

R: _____
What do you need to receive from God? His love, mercy, grace, comfort, or something else?

Write your favorite verse from today's reading here:

_____
_____

DAY 314:

Luke: Chapter 3
I John: Chapter 2
Ezekiel: Chapters 15-16
Psalm 133

H: _____
What gentle whisper did you hear as you read today?

E: _____
How did the passages encourage you?

A: _____
How can you apply what you learned in your day today?

R: _____
What do you need to receive from God? His love, mercy, grace, comfort, or something else?

Write your favorite verse from today's reading here:

_____
_____

DAILY PRAYER

Lord, help me hear Your gentle whispers as I read Your Word. Encourage me as I learn more about Your heart. Help me apply what I learn and act according to Your will. And help me receive all You have for me to receive from You today. In Jesus' name, Amen.

DAY 315:

Luke: Chapter 4
I John: Chapter 3
Ezekiel: Chapters 17-18
Psalm 134

H: _____
What gentle whisper did you hear as you read today?

E: _____
How did the passages encourage you?

A: _____
How can you apply what you learned in your day today?

R: _____
What do you need to receive from God? His love, mercy, grace, comfort, or something else?

Write your favorite verse from today's reading here:

_____

_____

DAY 316:

Luke: Chapter 5
I John: Chapter 4
Ezekiel: Chapters 19-20
Psalm 135

H: _____
What gentle whisper did you hear as you read today?

E: _____
How did the passages encourage you?

A: _____
How can you apply what you learned in your day today?

R: _____
What do you need to receive from God? His love, mercy, grace, comfort, or something else?

Write your favorite verse from today's reading here:

_____

_____

DAILY PRAYER

Lord, help me hear Your gentle whispers as I read Your Word. Encourage me as I learn more about Your heart. Help me apply what I learn and act according to Your will. And help me receive all You have for me to receive from You today. In Jesus' name, Amen.

DAY 317:

Luke: Chapter 6
I John: Chapter 5
Ezekiel: Chapters 21-22
Psalm 136

H: _____
What gentle whisper did you hear as you read today?

E: _____
How did the passages encourage you?

A: _____
How can you apply what you learned in your day today?

R: _____
What do you need to receive from God? His love, mercy, grace, comfort, or something else?

Write your favorite verse from today's reading here:

_____
_____

DAY 318:

Luke: Chapter 7
II John: Chapter 1
Ezekiel: Chapters 23-24
Psalm 137

H: _____
What gentle whisper did you hear as you read today?

E: _____
How did the passages encourage you?

A: _____
How can you apply what you learned in your day today?

R: _____
What do you need to receive from God? His love, mercy, grace, comfort, or something else?

Write your favorite verse from today's reading here:

_____
_____

DAILY PRAYER

Lord, help me hear Your gentle whispers as I read Your Word. Encourage me as I learn more about Your heart. Help me apply what I learn and act according to Your will. And help me receive all You have for me to receive from You today. In Jesus' name, Amen.

DAY 319:

Luke: Chapter 8
III John: Chapter 1
Ezekiel: Chapters 25-26
Psalm 138

H: _____
What gentle whisper did you hear as you read today?

E: _____
How did the passages encourage you?

A: _____
How can you apply what you learned in your day today?

R: _____
What do you need to receive from God? His love, mercy, grace, comfort, or something else?

Write your favorite verse from today's reading here:

_____

_____

DAY 320:

Luke: Chapter 9
Jude: Chapter 1
Ezekiel: Chapters 27-28
Psalm 139

H: _____
What gentle whisper did you hear as you read today?

E: _____
How did the passages encourage you?

A: _____
How can you apply what you learned in your day today?

R: _____
What do you need to receive from God? His love, mercy, grace, comfort, or something else?

Write your favorite verse from today's reading here:

_____

_____

DAILY PRAYER

Lord, help me hear Your gentle whispers as I read Your Word. Encourage me as I learn more about Your heart. Help me apply what I learn and act according to Your will. And help me receive all You have for me to receive from You today. In Jesus' name, Amen.

DAY 321:

Luke: Chapter 10
Revelation: Chapter 1
Ezekiel: Chapters 29-30
Psalm 140

H: _____
What gentle whisper did you hear as you read today?

E: _____
How did the passages encourage you?

A: _____
How can you apply what you learned in your day today?

R: _____
What do you need to receive from God? His love, mercy, grace, comfort, or something else?

Write your favorite verse from today's reading here:

_____

_____

DAY 322:

Luke: Chapter 11
Revelation: Chapter 2
Ezekiel: Chapters 31-32
Psalm 141

H: _____
What gentle whisper did you hear as you read today?

E: _____
How did the passages encourage you?

A: _____
How can you apply what you learned in your day today?

R: _____
What do you need to receive from God? His love, mercy, grace, comfort, or something else?

Write your favorite verse from today's reading here:

_____

_____

DAILY PRAYER

Lord, help me hear Your gentle whispers as I read Your Word. Encourage me as I learn more about Your heart. Help me apply what I learn and act according to Your will. And help me receive all You have for me to receive from You today. In Jesus' name, Amen.

DAY 323:

Luke: Chapter 12
Revelation: Chapter 3
Ezekiel: Chapters 33-34
Psalm 142

H: _____
What gentle whisper did you hear as you read today?

E: _____
How did the passages encourage you?

A: _____
How can you apply what you learned in your day today?

R: _____
What do you need to receive from God? His love, mercy, grace, comfort, or something else?

Write your favorite verse from today's reading here:

_____
_____

DAY 324:

Luke: Chapter 13
Revelation: Chapter 4
Ezekiel: Chapters 35-36
Psalm 143

H: _____
What gentle whisper did you hear as you read today?

E: _____
How did the passages encourage you?

A: _____
How can you apply what you learned in your day today?

R: _____
What do you need to receive from God? His love, mercy, grace, comfort, or something else?

Write your favorite verse from today's reading here:

_____
_____

DAILY PRAYER

Lord, help me hear Your gentle whispers as I read Your Word. Encourage me as I learn more about Your heart. Help me apply what I learn and act according to Your will. And help me receive all You have for me to receive from You today. In Jesus' name, Amen.

DAY 325:

Luke: Chapter 14
Revelation: Chapter 5
Ezekiel: Chapters 37-38
Psalm 144

H: _____
What gentle whisper did you hear as you read today?

E: _____
How did the passages encourage you?

A: _____
How can you apply what you learned in your day today?

R: _____
What do you need to receive from God? His love, mercy, grace, comfort, or something else?

Write your favorite verse from today's reading here:

_____

_____

DAY 326:

Luke: Chapter 15
Revelation: Chapter 6
Ezekiel: Chapters 39-40
Psalm 145

H: _____
What gentle whisper did you hear as you read today?

E: _____
How did the passages encourage you?

A: _____
How can you apply what you learned in your day today?

R: _____
What do you need to receive from God? His love, mercy, grace, comfort, or something else?

Write your favorite verse from today's reading here:

_____

_____

DAILY PRAYER

Lord, help me hear Your gentle whispers as I read Your Word. Encourage me as I learn more about Your heart. Help me apply what I learn and act according to Your will. And help me receive all You have for me to receive from You today. In Jesus' name, Amen.

DAY 327:

Luke: Chapter 16
Revelation: Chapter 7
Ezekiel: Chapters 41-42
Psalm 146

H: _____
What gentle whisper did you hear as you read today?

E: _____
How did the passages encourage you?

A: _____
How can you apply what you learned in your day today?

R: _____
What do you need to receive from God? His love, mercy, grace, comfort, or something else?

Write your favorite verse from today's reading here:

_____

_____

DAY 328:

Luke: Chapter 17
Revelation: Chapter 8
Ezekiel: Chapters 43-44
Psalm 147

H: _____
What gentle whisper did you hear as you read today?

E: _____
How did the passages encourage you?

A: _____
How can you apply what you learned in your day today?

R: _____
What do you need to receive from God? His love, mercy, grace, comfort, or something else?

Write your favorite verse from today's reading here:

_____

_____

DAILY PRAYER

Lord, help me hear Your gentle whispers as I read Your Word. Encourage me as I learn more about Your heart. Help me apply what I learn and act according to Your will. And help me receive all You have for me to receive from You today. In Jesus' name, Amen.

DAY 329:

Luke: Chapter 18
Revelation: Chapter 9
Ezekiel: Chapters 45-46
Psalm 148

H: _____
What gentle whisper did you hear as you read today?

E: _____
How did the passages encourage you?

A: _____
How can you apply what you learned in your day today?

R: _____
What do you need to receive from God? His love, mercy, grace, comfort, or something else?

Write your favorite verse from today's reading here:

_____

_____

DAY 330:

Luke: Chapter 19
Revelation: Chapter 10
Ezekiel: Chapters 47-48
Psalm 149

H: _____
What gentle whisper did you hear as you read today?

E: _____
How did the passages encourage you?

A: _____
How can you apply what you learned in your day today?

R: _____
What do you need to receive from God? His love, mercy, grace, comfort, or something else?

Write your favorite verse from today's reading here:

_____

_____

DAILY PRAYER

Lord, help me hear Your gentle whispers as I read Your Word. Encourage me as I learn more about Your heart. Help me apply what I learn and act according to Your will. And help me receive all You have for me to receive from You today. In Jesus' name, Amen.

DAY 331:

Luke: Chapter 20
Revelation: Chapter 11
Daniel: Chapters 1-2
Psalm 150

H: _____
What gentle whisper did you hear as you read today?

E: _____
How did the passages encourage you?

A: _____
How can you apply what you learned in your day today?

R: _____
What do you need to receive from God? His love, mercy, grace, comfort, or something else?

Write your favorite verse from today's reading here:

_____

_____

DAY 332:

Luke: Chapter 21
Revelation: Chapter 12
Daniel: Chapters 3-4
Proverbs 1

H: _____
What gentle whisper did you hear as you read today?

E: _____
How did the passages encourage you?

A: _____
How can you apply what you learned in your day today?

R: _____
What do you need to receive from God? His love, mercy, grace, comfort, or something else?

Write your favorite verse from today's reading here:

_____

_____

DAILY PRAYER

Lord, help me hear Your gentle whispers as I read Your Word. Encourage me as I learn more about Your heart. Help me apply what I learn and act according to Your will. And help me receive all You have for me to receive from You today. In Jesus' name, Amen.

DAY 333:

Luke: Chapter 22
Revelation: Chapter 13
Daniel: Chapters 5-6
Proverbs 2

H: _____
What gentle whisper did you hear as you read today?

E: _____
How did the passages encourage you?

A: _____
How can you apply what you learned in your day today?

R: _____
What do you need to receive from God? His love, mercy, grace, comfort, or something else?

Write your favorite verse from today's reading here:

_____

_____

DAY 334:

Luke: Chapter 23
Revelation: Chapter 14
Daniel: Chapters 7-8
Proverbs 3

H: _____
What gentle whisper did you hear as you read today?

E: _____
How did the passages encourage you?

A: _____
How can you apply what you learned in your day today?

R: _____
What do you need to receive from God? His love, mercy, grace, comfort, or something else?

Write your favorite verse from today's reading here:

_____

_____

DAILY PRAYER

Lord, help me hear Your gentle whispers as I read Your Word. Encourage me as I learn more about Your heart. Help me apply what I learn and act according to Your will. And help me receive all You have for me to receive from You today. In Jesus' name, Amen.

DAY 335:

Luke: Chapter 24
Revelation: Chapter 15
Daniel: Chapters 9-10
Proverbs 4

H: _____
What gentle whisper did you hear as you read today?

E: _____
How did the passages encourage you?

A: _____
How can you apply what you learned in your day today?

R: _____
What do you need to receive from God? His love, mercy, grace, comfort, or something else?

Write your favorite verse from today's reading here:

_____
_____

DAY 336:

John: Chapter 1
Revelation: Chapter 16
Daniel: Chapters 11-12
Proverbs 5

H: _____
What gentle whisper did you hear as you read today?

E: _____
How did the passages encourage you?

A: _____
How can you apply what you learned in your day today?

R: _____
What do you need to receive from God? His love, mercy, grace, comfort, or something else?

Write your favorite verse from today's reading here:

_____
_____

DAILY PRAYER

Lord, help me hear Your gentle whispers as I read Your Word. Encourage me as I learn more about Your heart. Help me apply what I learn and act according to Your will. And help me receive all You have for me to receive from You today. In Jesus' name, Amen.

DAY 337:

John: Chapter 2
Revelation: Chapter 17
Hosea: Chapters 1-2
Proverbs 6

H: _____
What gentle whisper did you hear as you read today?

E: _____
How did the passages encourage you?

A: _____
How can you apply what you learned in your day today?

R: _____
What do you need to receive from God? His love, mercy, grace, comfort, or something else?

Write your favorite verse from today's reading here:

_____

_____

DAY 338:

John: Chapter 3
Revelation: Chapter 18
Hosea: Chapters 3-4
Proverbs 7

H: _____
What gentle whisper did you hear as you read today?

E: _____
How did the passages encourage you?

A: _____
How can you apply what you learned in your day today?

R: _____
What do you need to receive from God? His love, mercy, grace, comfort, or something else?

Write your favorite verse from today's reading here:

_____

_____

DAILY PRAYER

Lord, help me hear Your gentle whispers as I read Your Word. Encourage me as I learn more about Your heart. Help me apply what I learn and act according to Your will. And help me receive all You have for me to receive from You today. In Jesus' name, Amen.

DAY 339:

John: Chapter 4
Revelation: Chapter 19
Hosea: Chapters 5-6
Proverbs 8

H: _____
What gentle whisper did you hear as you read today?

E: _____
How did the passages encourage you?

A: _____
How can you apply what you learned in your day today?

R: _____
What do you need to receive from God? His love, mercy, grace, comfort, or something else?

Write your favorite verse from today's reading here:

_____

_____

DAY 340:

John: Chapter 5
Revelation: Chapter 20
Hosea: Chapters 7-8
Proverbs 9

H: _____
What gentle whisper did you hear as you read today?

E: _____
How did the passages encourage you?

A: _____
How can you apply what you learned in your day today?

R: _____
What do you need to receive from God? His love, mercy, grace, comfort, or something else?

Write your favorite verse from today's reading here:

_____

_____

DAILY PRAYER

Lord, help me hear Your gentle whispers as I read Your Word. Encourage me as I learn more about Your heart. Help me apply what I learn and act according to Your will. And help me receive all You have for me to receive from You today. In Jesus' name, Amen.

DAY 341:

John: Chapter 6
Revelation: Chapter 21
Hosea: Chapters 9-10
Proverbs 10

H: _____
What gentle whisper did you hear as you read today?

E: _____
How did the passages encourage you?

A: _____
How can you apply what you learned in your day today?

R: _____
What do you need to receive from God? His love, mercy, grace, comfort, or something else?

Write your favorite verse from today's reading here:

_____
_____

DAY 342:

John: Chapter 7
Revelation: Chapter 22
Hosea: Chapters 11-12
Proverbs 11

H: _____
What gentle whisper did you hear as you read today?

E: _____
How did the passages encourage you?

A: _____
How can you apply what you learned in your day today?

R: _____
What do you need to receive from God? His love, mercy, grace, comfort, or something else?

Write your favorite verse from today's reading here:

_____
_____

DAILY PRAYER

Lord, help me hear Your gentle whispers as I read Your Word. Encourage me as I learn more about Your heart. Help me apply what I learn and act according to Your will. And help me receive all You have for me to receive from You today. In Jesus' name, Amen.

DAY 343:

John: Chapter 8
Hosea: Chapters 13-14
Proverbs 12

H: _____
What gentle whisper did you hear as you read today?

E: _____
How did the passages encourage you?

A: _____
How can you apply what you learned in your day today?

R: _____
What do you need to receive from God? His love, mercy, grace, comfort, or something else?

Write your favorite verse from today's reading here:

_____
_____

DAY 344:

John: Chapter 9
Joel: Chapters 1-3
Proverbs 13

H: _____
What gentle whisper did you hear as you read today?

E: _____
How did the passages encourage you?

A: _____
How can you apply what you learned in your day today?

R: _____
What do you need to receive from God? His love, mercy, grace, comfort, or something else?

Write your favorite verse from today's reading here:

_____
_____

DAILY PRAYER

Lord, help me hear Your gentle whispers as I read Your Word. Encourage me as I learn more about Your heart. Help me apply what I learn and act according to Your will. And help me receive all You have for me to receive from You today. In Jesus' name, Amen.

DAY 345:

John: Chapter 10
Amos: Chapters 1-2
Proverbs 14

H: _____
What gentle whisper did you hear as you read today?

E: _____
How did the passages encourage you?

A: _____
How can you apply what you learned in your day today?

R: _____
What do you need to receive from God? His love, mercy, grace, comfort, or something else?

Write your favorite verse from today's reading here:

_____

_____

DAY 346:

John: Chapter 11
Amos: Chapters 3-4
Proverbs 15

H: _____
What gentle whisper did you hear as you read today?

E: _____
How did the passages encourage you?

A: _____
How can you apply what you learned in your day today?

R: _____
What do you need to receive from God? His love, mercy, grace, comfort, or something else?

Write your favorite verse from today's reading here:

_____

_____

DAILY PRAYER

Lord, help me hear Your gentle whispers as I read Your Word. Encourage me as I learn more about Your heart. Help me apply what I learn and act according to Your will. And help me receive all You have for me to receive from You today. In Jesus' name, Amen.

DAY 347:

John: Chapter 12
Amos: Chapters 5-6
Proverbs 16

H: _____
What gentle whisper did you hear as you read today?

E: _____
How did the passages encourage you?

A: _____
How can you apply what you learned in your day today?

R: _____
What do you need to receive from God? His love, mercy, grace, comfort, or something else?

Write your favorite verse from today's reading here:

_____

_____

DAY 348:

John: Chapter 13
Amos: Chapters 7-9
Proverbs 17

H: _____
What gentle whisper did you hear as you read today?

E: _____
How did the passages encourage you?

A: _____
How can you apply what you learned in your day today?

R: _____
What do you need to receive from God? His love, mercy, grace, comfort, or something else?

Write your favorite verse from today's reading here:

_____

_____

DAILY PRAYER

Lord, help me hear Your gentle whispers as I read Your Word. Encourage me as I learn more about Your heart. Help me apply what I learn and act according to Your will. And help me receive all You have for me to receive from You today. In Jesus' name, Amen.

DAY 349:

John: Chapter 14
Obadiah: Chapter 1
Jonah: Chapters 1-2
Proverbs 18

H: _____
What gentle whisper did you hear as you read today?

E: _____
How did the passages encourage you?

A: _____
How can you apply what you learned in your day today?

R: _____
What do you need to receive from God? His love, mercy, grace, comfort, or something else?

Write your favorite verse from today's reading here:

_____

_____

DAY 350:

John: Chapter 15
Jonah: Chapters 3-4
Proverbs 19

H: _____
What gentle whisper did you hear as you read today?

E: _____
How did the passages encourage you?

A: _____
How can you apply what you learned in your day today?

R: _____
What do you need to receive from God? His love, mercy, grace, comfort, or something else?

Write your favorite verse from today's reading here:

_____

_____

DAILY PRAYER

Lord, help me hear Your gentle whispers as I read Your Word. Encourage me as I learn more about Your heart. Help me apply what I learn and act according to Your will. And help me receive all You have for me to receive from You today. In Jesus' name, Amen.

DAY 351:

John: Chapter 16
Micah: Chapters 1-2
Proverbs 20

H: _____
What gentle whisper did you hear as you read today?

E: _____
How did the passages encourage you?

A: _____
How can you apply what you learned in your day today?

R: _____
What do you need to receive from God? His love, mercy, grace, comfort, or something else?

Write your favorite verse from today's reading here:

_____
_____

DAY 352:

John: Chapter 17
Micah: Chapters 3-4
Proverbs 21

H: _____
What gentle whisper did you hear as you read today?

E: _____
How did the passages encourage you?

A: _____
How can you apply what you learned in your day today?

R: _____
What do you need to receive from God? His love, mercy, grace, comfort, or something else?

Write your favorite verse from today's reading here:

_____
_____

DAILY PRAYER

Lord, help me hear Your gentle whispers as I read Your Word. Encourage me as I learn more about Your heart. Help me apply what I learn and act according to Your will. And help me receive all You have for me to receive from You today. In Jesus' name, Amen.

DAY 353:

John: Chapter 18
Micah: Chapters 5-7
Proverbs 22

H: _____
What gentle whisper did you hear as you read today?

E: _____
How did the passages encourage you?

A: _____
How can you apply what you learned in your day today?

R: _____
What do you need to receive from God? His love, mercy, grace, comfort, or something else?

Write your favorite verse from today's reading here:

_____

_____

DAY 354:

John: Chapter 19
Nahum: Chapters 1-3
Proverbs 23

H: _____
What gentle whisper did you hear as you read today?

E: _____
How did the passages encourage you?

A: _____
How can you apply what you learned in your day today?

R: _____
What do you need to receive from God? His love, mercy, grace, comfort, or something else?

Write your favorite verse from today's reading here:

_____

_____

DAILY PRAYER

Lord, help me hear Your gentle whispers as I read Your Word. Encourage me as I learn more about Your heart. Help me apply what I learn and act according to Your will. And help me receive all You have for me to receive from You today. In Jesus' name, Amen.

DAY 355:

John: Chapter 20
Habakkuk: Chapters 1-3
Proverbs 24

H: _____
What gentle whisper did you hear as you read today?

E: _____
How did the passages encourage you?

A: _____
How can you apply what you learned in your day today?

R: _____
What do you need to receive from God? His love, mercy, grace, comfort, or something else?

Write your favorite verse from today's reading here:

_____

_____

DAY 356:

John: Chapter 21
Zephaniah: Chapters 1-3
Proverbs 25

H: _____
What gentle whisper did you hear as you read today?

E: _____
How did the passages encourage you?

A: _____
How can you apply what you learned in your day today?

R: _____
What do you need to receive from God? His love, mercy, grace, comfort, or something else?

Write your favorite verse from today's reading here:

_____

_____

DAILY PRAYER

Lord, help me hear Your gentle whispers as I read Your Word. Encourage me as I learn more about Your heart. Help me apply what I learn and act according to Your will. And help me receive all You have for me to receive from You today. In Jesus' name, Amen.

DAY 357:

Haggai: Chapters 1-2
Proverbs 26

H: _____
What gentle whisper did you hear as you read today?

E: _____
How did the passages encourage you?

A: _____
How can you apply what you learned in your day today?

R: _____
What do you need to receive from God? His love, mercy, grace, comfort, or something else?

Write your favorite verse from today's reading here:

_____
_____

DAY 358:

Zechariah: Chapters 1-2
Proverbs 27

H: _____
What gentle whisper did you hear as you read today?

E: _____
How did the passages encourage you?

A: _____
How can you apply what you learned in your day today?

R: _____
What do you need to receive from God? His love, mercy, grace, comfort, or something else?

Write your favorite verse from today's reading here:

_____
_____

DAILY PRAYER

Lord, help me hear Your gentle whispers as I read Your Word. Encourage me as I learn more about Your heart. Help me apply what I learn and act according to Your will. And help me receive all You have for me to receive from You today. In Jesus' name, Amen.

DAY 359:

Zechariah: Chapters 3-4
Proverbs 28

H: _____
What gentle whisper did you hear as you read today?

E: _____
How did the passages encourage you?

A: _____
How can you apply what you learned in your day today?

R: _____
What do you need to receive from God? His love, mercy, grace, comfort, or something else?

Write your favorite verse from today's reading here:

_____

_____

DAY 360:

Zechariah: Chapters 5-6
Proverbs 29

H: _____
What gentle whisper did you hear as you read today?

E: _____
How did the passages encourage you?

A: _____
How can you apply what you learned in your day today?

R: _____
What do you need to receive from God? His love, mercy, grace, comfort, or something else?

Write your favorite verse from today's reading here:

_____

_____

DAILY PRAYER

Lord, help me hear Your gentle whispers as I read Your Word. Encourage me as I learn more about Your heart. Help me apply what I learn and act according to Your will. And help me receive all You have for me to receive from You today. In Jesus' name, Amen.

DAY 361:

Zechariah: Chapters 7-8
Proverbs 30

H: _____
What gentle whisper did you hear as you read today?

E: _____
How did the passages encourage you?

A: _____
How can you apply what you learned in your day today?

R: _____
What do you need to receive from God? His love, mercy, grace, comfort, or something else?

Write your favorite verse from today's reading here:

_____
_____

DAY 362:

Zechariah: Chapters 9-10
Proverbs 31

H: _____
What gentle whisper did you hear as you read today?

E: _____
How did the passages encourage you?

A: _____
How can you apply what you learned in your day today?

R: _____
What do you need to receive from God? His love, mercy, grace, comfort, or something else?

Write your favorite verse from today's reading here:

_____
_____

DAILY PRAYER

Lord, help me hear Your gentle whispers as I read Your Word. Encourage me as I learn more about Your heart. Help me apply what I learn and act according to Your will. And help me receive all You have for me to receive from You today. In Jesus' name, Amen.

DAY 363:

Zechariah: Chapters 11-12

H: _____
What gentle whisper did you hear as you read today?

E: _____
How did the passages encourage you?

A: _____
How can you apply what you learned in your day today?

R: _____
What do you need to receive from God? His love, mercy, grace, comfort, or something else?

Write your favorite verse from today's reading here:

_____

_____

DAY 364

Zechariah: Chapters 13-14

H: _____
What gentle whisper did you hear as you read today?

E: _____
How did the passages encourage you?

A: _____
How can you apply what you learned in your day today?

R: _____
What do you need to receive from God? His love, mercy, grace, comfort, or something else?

Write your favorite verse from today's reading here:

_____

_____

DAILY PRAYER

Lord, help me hear Your gentle whispers as I read Your Word. Encourage me as I learn more about Your heart. Help me apply what I learn and act according to Your will. And help me receive all You have for me to receive from You today. In Jesus' name, Amen.

DAY 365

Malachi: Chapters 1-4

H: _____
What gentle whisper did you hear as you read today?

E: _____
How did the passages encourage you?

A: _____
How can you apply what you learned in your day today?

R: _____
What do you need to receive from God? His love, mercy, grace, comfort, or something else?

Write your favorite verse from today's reading here:

_____

_____

ABOUT THE AUTHOR

Andrea Lende is an author of several books including 90 Day Prayer Journal: Drawing Closer to God, God's Whispers and Melodies: A Heart Transformed Through Music and Lyrics, and God is Still Almighty: 90 Daily Devotions. Her writing instills hope, gratefulness, and strength to her readers. She is also a speaker, and host of Downloads from God podcast. She encourages and inspires women to draw closer to God and learn more of His ways. She lives near Denver and is mother to three adult sons. You can follow Andrea and her online ministry at www.BelievingHim.com.